ANGER 101

The Healthy Approach to Being a Bitch

LORI DIGUARDI

Copyright © 2017 Lori DiGuardi.

All rights reserved. No part of this book may be reproduced, stored, or transmitted by any means—whether auditory, graphic, mechanical, or electronic—without written permission of both publisher and author, except in the case of brief excerpts used in critical articles and reviews. Unauthorized reproduction of any part of this work is illegal and is punishable by law.

ISBN: 978-1-4834-6489-3 (sc)
ISBN: 978-1-4834-6488-6 (e)

Library of Congress Control Number: 2017901225

Because of the dynamic nature of the Internet, any web addresses or links contained in this book may have changed since publication and may no longer be valid. The views expressed in this work are solely those of the author and do not necessarily reflect the views of the publisher, and the publisher hereby disclaims any responsibility for them.

Any people depicted in stock imagery provided by Thinkstock are models, and such images are being used for illustrative purposes only.
Certain stock imagery © Thinkstock.

Lulu Publishing Services rev. date: 02/21/2017

For my mother

The truth of your life
Pulses through eternity
Shouting "Yes, Yes, Yes!"

Table of Contents

Preface ix

Introduction xxi

In the Beginning 1

The Truth about Anger 6

On Being a Bitch 22

Living the Lie 40

Conscious Choice and Courage 56

Honoring the Truth 68

Blaming Others 84

Love That Moves Mountains 99

Letting Go 111

An Enriched Life 125

Starting Over 140

Conclusion 147

A Prayer for the Remembrance of Truth 155

Acknowledgments 157

About the Author 159

Preface

Despite what many on the spiritual path believe, anger is necessary for enlightenment.

Anger 101 presents this emotion as the healthy and sacred energy it is. Anger and all of our emotional energies are natural and serve a vital function. They exist because we exist; to ignore any of them is to ignore the inner expression of our very existence. Our inner expression vitally guides us onto a journey of authentic power and truth.

At any given moment, how we feel is the truth of our existence. And we have a right to how we feel. Responding to the moment by honoring our inner truth results in integrity in thought, word, and deed. *Anger 101* helps us recognize, acknowledge, and honor this inner voice of anger, making it okay to heed its wisdom.

Our bodies create emotional energy to guide us through each moment. Responding wisely and authentically to the moment provides the gateway to a life of emotional integrity. *Anger 101* presents *my* struggle with anger, how the struggle formed, and how I became liberated from the grasp anger had on me.

Liberation is a journey into emotional integrity, a life in which every cell of our being shouts, "Yes!" to our deepest and infinite truth. Emotional integrity is required for a self-loving, soulful, and spiritually fulfilling life.

These pages present my experience of how living in the trenches of my humanness *with Embodied Awareness and emotional integrity* have led to my greatest truths. My journey delves into loving the blessing and miracle of my own truth—my path to self-love.

The All of Us

To authentically love ourselves and create our greatest lives, we must embrace the *all* of us. That isn't easy to do in this world where certain things are judged as *bad* and others judged as *good*. When we judge the natural expressions of our humanness as *bad*, we prevent ourselves from creating the life of our dreams. When we make how we feel wrong, we make ourselves wrong, for it's our inner truth. When we seemingly go in circles with our lives, run into dead ends, or find ourselves repeating unacceptable circumstances, we need to take heed.

It means we're being shown that we're shut off from our inner truth—for the healthy, emotional energy of anger would never guide us down those paths.

It's the *misperceptions* about its meaning that give anger a bad rap. And with so many negative misperceptions, it's no wonder we struggle to find our authentic voice and honor it with actions of emotional integrity.

Change the Perception

Anger 101 aims to change the perception of both anger and being a bitch in a truthful, positive, life-affirming way—one that feels wonderful and expansive and exciting. Living a life of emotional integrity and guided by inner truth is as juicy a life as one can live.

Yet to get to the point of being in emotional integrity takes guidance, practice, and tons of patience and self-love. If it were easy, we'd all be living joyfully and peacefully. But we humans seem to need a lot of convincing that we are *worthy* just because we are *alive*.

What we learn in our early years, for better or worse, sticks to us like Velcro. What we learn about *ourselves*—that who we are isn't enough, who we are is wrong, and what we feel isn't valid—simply isn't true.

This untruth misguided me for more than thirty years. I aspired for more but kept running in circles and hitting dead ends. Finally, I learned the healthy approach to being a bitch. And today, I live with emotional integrity grounded along the path of enlightenment. This doesn't mean I'm a Buddha, but I *am* ever closer to embodying my Buddhahood because I'm finally embodying the *all* of me.

Own Your Awesomeness

Through this book, I'm here to give you permission to *own your awesomeness*. Let go of the "less than" belief you probably have about yourself. Ultimately, you have a permission slip to prioritize your inner truth above all else.

A serious car accident inspired me to start writing this book five years ago. Expressing anger became part of my whiplash recovery program. The words that formed as I pounded on the keyboard begged me to give attention to whatever aspect of my life needed *me* the most: my inner truth.

Thankfully, after four months of intensive holistic healthcare, I started feeling better. Life as usual resumed and the backlog of responsibilities from an overburdened life—one in which my inner truth was not a priority—once again became status quo. So I stopped writing this manuscript and shoved my inner voice of anger into a passive, painful silence that I knew only too well.

Fortunately, my overburdened life became too suffocating to continue. By the end of 2015, my inner truth came closer than ever to holding the number one spot on my priority list. I sold my house and my belongings, resigned from my board positions, bought a red two-seater sports car, and moved across the country.

Given this profound choice, several people asked if I was going through a mid-life crisis. This question surprised me, but I understood their curiosity. I knew I was simply ready to be free from a life that didn't honor my true self. The timing seemed right to *choose freedom*.

True freedom always requires conscious choice. For me, that meant a complete transformation of life as I knew it. So as a response to the question "Are you going through a mid-life crisis," I'd respond, "No, I am going through a conscious life transformation."

Since then, my transformational choice has opened the door to a vibrant life—a life in which my inner truth is my passion, my North Star. I was and am committed to freedom and truth. And as always, once a commitment is made, anything that stands in its way shows up and demands attention.

Give Truth Center Stage

As soon as I became somewhat settled in my new home, I set a goal to give my inner truth center stage—literally. I do powerful presentation work on stage, so I set a goal to create transformational speaking opportunities. It was then I learned that TEDx Tucson was accepting applications for its next event. I decided to apply.

First I had to answer the questions TEDx asks of potential speakers: "What idea of yours is worth sharing and why? What idea of yours deserves to be on the TEDx stage? What idea of yours is radical and unique?"

To answer these questions meant looking deeply into my life's journey. I reflected on the past twenty years of my work in America, Europe, and Africa in the corporate and non-profit sectors as well as being a personal development coach. I mentally scanned all of the speeches, presentations, and workshops I had given over the years. And then I remembered the manuscript I started five years ago—the one about anger that had remained dormant on the hard drive of my computer.

But as soon as I remembered this manuscript, it whispered, "Give me life, Lori." I pulled it out of storage, reread what I had written, and found the answer to TEDx's "what idea?" question. Then I submitted the TEDx application.

On the day of the TEDx audition and before my turn on the round red carpet, people at the event asked me, "What's your talk about?" Even though I had lived the theme of my life and this talk for years, I still felt apprehensive about speaking my truth—and sharing it. In response, each time I'd take a breath, straighten my posture, and exhale my answer. "The title of my talk is Anger 101: The Healthy Approach to Being a Bitch."

After answering, I felt relaxed yet curious with a tinge of excitement. Then I'd smile and wait for their response. Raised eyebrows. Every time. This confirmed that at least my title was radical, unique, and perhaps intriguing.

When my audition talk was over that day, I mingled with the crowd and received surprising responses. People offered congratulations and, more than that, they thanked me. Their raised eyebrows were replaced with open eyes and open hearts.

My talk had resonated with them. It told me that addressing the true nature of anger spoke to the true nature of people hungry for acknowledgment and honor. That is, we need to *know we matter* and aren't the only ones dealing with that issue.

I know a lot about honoring the inner truth of anger. I live that now. I also know a lot about *not* honoring the inner truth of anger—the traumas and hardships of life when inner truth is ignored. I had lived that way for almost half my life.

Specifically, I lived as a victim for almost three decades. When I was repeatedly thrown into the trenches of despair, I wondered if life was worth all the suffering. Yet I never gave up on it. I was born with great resilience and the knowledge that life offered more, even if I didn't have a clue what that "more" could be. But I could *feel* it, and I *wanted* it.

A Source of Strength

At her 2009 presentation given in my community, I experienced Gerda Weissmann Klein, a holocaust survivor and human rights activist. Gerda's presence was powerful. Every word she breathed life into was filled with wisdom, strength, and love. From her message, I wrote down this statement: "Pain should not be wasted. You assuage your own pain. You never forget, but the memory lodges in a different space and becomes a source of strength." Mrs. Klein's source of strength is the foundation for her work.

The pain I experienced in my life is also a source of strength—and now the foundation for my work, too. Sharing it is both an obligation and a privilege.

My life is my message. I tell my story to acknowledge the unspoken hunger that exists in others and maybe in you. I share hoping my story becomes a source of strength for those walking a similar path.

But mostly I write these words to give myself permission to be *me* as I was then and as I am now—perfect in all my imperfections. Indeed, I craft this whole book to give hope, permission, and voice to the inner truth of those who read it as well as to the one writing it.

Through my writing, I am learning where in my life I'm still not comfortable with my truth. This learning affords me the opportunity to continue to give myself permission to show up just as I am. For that, I am thankful.

How Humans Work

How I interpreted my life experiences as a child formed my subconscious beliefs. That's true for all of us. It's the way we humans work.

Our subconscious beliefs are a dominant force in the lives we create. The dominant negative subconscious beliefs formed from my childhood experiences are:

1) I am wrong just being me;
2) I get punished for just being me;
3) I must do whatever I can to *not* disappoint others (even if that means I disappoint myself);
4) Other people's wellbeing is more important than mine;
5) The truth doesn't matter;
6) It isn't safe to be me;
7) Sex is repulsive;
8) I don't matter;
9) It's always my fault;
10) I have to do what I can to make people feel comfortable.

Perhaps some of these subconscious beliefs resonate with you. They were reinforced in my teenage and early adult years as if a relay team passed the baton of false beliefs one person to the next until I was conditioned to carry on the tradition all by myself. These subconscious beliefs contributed to the greatest struggle of my life.

Subconscious beliefs are always in the driver's seat. However, unraveling the false beliefs is a key to freedom.

My Home Life

In my formative years, I inherited the archetypes of the silent child and victim conditioned into ignoring my truth, needs, and dreams. I suffered physical, verbal, and sexual abuse. Mostly, I learned anger from my parents. My father's anger erupted fast and fiercely in the form of physical punishment. My mother's anger was pushed down into her being until it became a painful passive silence. As a child, what I perceived as anger was awful, traumatic, and wrong. That meaning was literally beaten into me, and I learned to accept it, expect it, and be silent about it.

My parents divorced before I turned thirteen. With no father around and a mother whose voice remained silent, my teenage years turned out to be more traumatic than my early childhood. My mother's first boyfriend didn't like me—not one bit. He made it clear I did *not* belong, which made my home life a prison of insults and rejection. I spent time trying to belong somewhere, anywhere, but home. When I was fifteen, that being "anywhere but home" put me in an environment in which two "friends" of my older sister raped me—together.

I felt ashamed and pretended it never happened.

When I was sixteen, my mother remarried, and my new stepfather was an alcoholic. Unlike my mother's first boyfriend, my stepfather liked me a lot. Too much. As soon as we became a family under one roof, he forced sexual directives at me. He would corner me when my mother wasn't home, often in the basement laundry room. He would walk naked into my bedroom when he felt like it and invited me to join in his repulsive imaginings.

Again, I stayed away from home as much as possible.

Abusive Boyfriend and Boss

When I was still a teenager, I moved in with my first long-term boyfriend. No sooner had we started living together that I learned he was a drug addict. I also learned that physical and mental abuse were part of my new home. Because this pattern of life was strongly familiar, I stayed. With him, I endured several years of being beaten, choked, and imprisoned.

When I'd finally had enough, I ended the relationship. In response, he bought a gun. I left quickly while he was at work and took only my clothing, two cats, and the scar on my face from when he chased me into a glass window and refused to let me get medical attention.

Then, in my late twenties, I was employed by a man who was verbally abusive. Five of us worked in a two-room small city office. Yes, two male bosses and three young women. One of the bosses worked directly with us and verbally assaulted the three of us every day. The pattern I experienced with him was this: Nothing I did satisfied him; I did everything wrong (though I completed my tasks correctly and on time); I worked harder and harder. Still, I couldn't win his approval or stop his tyranny. One morning he made one of my colleagues cry *again*, and by lunchtime, I knew that was it. I'd had enough. I quit.

The colleague who had cried that morning asked me, "What if you can't find another job?" My response came more clearly to me than anything I'd ever said before in my life. "I don't care about that. I will not spend another second of my life being abused."

My Healing Journey Starts

From that moment onward, I was determined to understand and heal whatever had led me into traumatic life experiences time and again. My journey into self-love began.

Despite being born into victimhood, I am grateful because, unlike other people in similar instances, I didn't end up dead, handicapped, diseased, pregnant, a drug addict, or a criminal. I know I had a bevy of angels who protected me from the very worst abuse over the years. With their help and a growing awareness, I was able to break the disempowering legacy of my family's lineage.

The first half of my life was horrible, but I realize it could have been worse. The thing is, *I am an old soul*. My soul chose this life so I could understand the path of the silent child and victim, overcome it, and share my strength with others. The way it was meant to be.

I have no regrets. Life can be tough and complex, for being human is never easy. That's why it helps to be gentle with ourselves. Old habits take a while to replace, but they *are* replaceable. I have done it by transforming my subconscious beliefs and heeding my inner truth. And the work to accomplish that has become my passion.

Because of my conscious effort and knowing myself, these days I'm good at listening to my anger and all other emotional energies. Sometimes I still get tripped up in the drama, but mostly I honor my inner wisdom. The victim and silent child are long gone; they are my history but not my present or future.

It's still easy to get into my head and "go mental" at the first sense of bodily discomfort. Writing this manuscript has given me a perfect example of staying present and knowing I'm "good enough."

How many days can a person spend rewriting one paragraph to get it perfect to avoid disappointing people and be judged as a shitty writer? How many days? Lots of them.

But now, I'm okay if I'm considered a shitty writer. Why? Because writing this manuscript is my practice of showing up as *me* and trusting I'm an awesome person no matter what. I am, after all, writing this book for me.

 *If I can't be good enough for myself, it means I'm still holding the baton of lies handed to me from my early years.*

A Practice in "Being Me"

Consider this book a practice in just *being me* and being aware of what trips me up. Embodied Awareness is a practice. Showing up just as myself, however that looks, yet knowing I'm okay is a practice. And yet, I am living a soulful, self-loving, and fulfilling life.

I've known women who have been violated by strangers, their husbands, their sons, their mothers, their grandparents, their bosses, and their brothers. I've known women who have lost their children through parental alienation by abusive husbands. I've also known women who haven't suffered abuse or violence by others, and yet they still dishonor themselves by disassociating with their feelings. They prioritize other people over themselves. They are depressed, unhappy, and unfulfilled.

I know anger well—both the inner natural human emotion and the extreme outer reaction that gives anger a bad rap. In my coaching, I have helped women get in touch with their anger and supported them through a transformational journey into creating a more fulfilling life.

During my master's degree research, I studied the nervous system as well as stress and neuroscience. I now understand why false beliefs can have a hold on us from a biological perspective. My working knowledge of the science explains why we can override our emotions. From studying psychology and understanding the basics of our subconscious, I know which parts of the brain are active when we feel angry.

I've also explored acupuncture, Reiki, tapping, NET, shamanism, astrology, esoteric psychology, dousing, somatic therapy, African traditional healing, homeopathy, flower essences, professional coaching, dream therapy, affirmations, meditation, channeling, intuition, the tarot, and the Body and Emotion Code. I've swum with wild dolphins and chanted mantras, all in an effort to "Know Thyself," as Socrates said.

After a lifelong pursuit of getting to know myself, what I know today is this: A person doesn't need to study the science of anger, neurology, or stress; travel to Africa; be abused; wear the archetype of the silent child or victim; practice dozens of healing modalities; get a psychic reading or become a psychic; attend a TEDx talk; or even read this book to *honor the inner truth of anger*. Anyone can make anger an *ally* in creating a fulfilling life—without doing all the things I did.

Ultimately, nothing on the *outside* of us can replace the wisdom on the *inside* of us. Yet, from time to time, we all can use a helping hand to point us in the direction of the treasure we seek.

Inner Truth of Anger

Whatever treasure you may be seeking, this much is clear: *Your inner truth will guide you to your promised land.* And your inner truth of *anger* will guide you to a life that's soulful, self-loving, and fulfilling.

It's time to honor the truth of your existence. That's what my life is about. My hope is that my experience and my soul's wisdom presented on these pages become helping hands along *your* journey.

Join me in celebrating the inner truth of anger together.

Introduction

This is my story.

Within the covers of this book, I share my life experiences and soul wisdom. I'm not looking for accolades or approval from anyone other than myself. And neither should you. Your story is yours. Your truth is yours. What you experience in your precious life is sacred, and I need not try to convince you that your life should be different.

However, if you find that my story resonates with yours and you're wondering how you can create a soulful, self-loving, and deeply fulfilling life, perhaps what has worked for me can also work for you.

I used to say, "I've spent my entire life trying to be a bitch." I was joking on the surface but deep beneath the heartache from being victimized, I was serious. Not having a voice or a choice is an awful way to live. Not being connected to inner truth is a guaranteed way to stay powerless.

Yet when I learned it was possible to be a powerful me, nothing could stand in my way. I learned to connect with my inner truth of anger and found my voice. Today, I don't need to *try* to be a bitch any more. My life works; I have true power.

In fact, I'm delightfully surprised and grateful that my life is wonderful considering how *not* wonderful it was for so long. Conveying my "not wonderful" life experiences through this book was quite a tumultuous task. The writing triggered subconscious beliefs and old emotional energy that were hanging on and begging to be acknowledged. When they showed up, I took that as an opportunity to expand into more truth and power.

Subconscious Beliefs Triggered

Four main subconscious beliefs were triggered while writing this book. They presented themselves in the following questions I asked myself repeatedly:

1) "Does this stuff really matter?" Subconscious translation: "I don't matter."
2) "What if I really suck at writing?" Subconscious translation: "People are going to judge me."
3) "Who am I to share wisdom?" Subconscious translation: "I'm not good enough."
4) "What if the people in my stories recognize themselves?" Subconscious translation: "I'm responsible for the wellbeing of others."

Soon after they popped into my consciousness (but not soon enough for my own comfort), I saw those questions for what they were: fear. It was if I were playing poker and fear kept calling my bluff. Fortunately, my hand is my truth and fear could not force me to fold.

The truth is this: "Of course my stories and wisdom are important. Who cares if I suck at writing? I don't. I'm a wise woman, and I'm not responsible for the wellbeing of others."

Transform Old Energy

Many days while writing about painful experiences, I wanted to quit. I still had emotional energy from previous traumas that needed love and acknowledgment—such as when Buddy protected me, a biggee event, bless his soul. (See the story about my dog Buddy in the chapter "The Truth about Anger".)

Writing helped me transform that old energy once and for all. It gave me ample opportunity to practice Embodied Awareness and the Acknowledgment Cycle—both practices I suggest in this book.

At the end of each chapter, you'll find encouragement to do these two practices:

1) Embodied Awareness
2) Acknowledgment Cycle

Their purpose is to help you *feel* the truth within you—and to *acknowledge* and *honor* your truth.

The prerequisite for learning this healthy approach to being a bitch is to connect to the anger within you. When you connect with this healthy emotional energy of anger, you can acknowledge it, honor it, and let it guide you with its wisdom. This process provides the path for a fulfilling life and the way to emotional and spiritual maturity. *This process is the only way.*

Writing this book was all about me; reading this book is all about you. Trust yourself always. No one is more important than you.

HOW TO USE THIS BOOK

At the end of each chapter is a section called TIME FOR YOUR TRUTH. There, I suggest practicing the Grounding Exercise (see description that follows) before and after you read and answer the questions in the section. By grounding yourself in your body and getting present, your energy will guide you to the answers most wanting to be revealed.

This practice is not about being in your head. With Embodied Awareness, your inner power grows, and you can better unravel your subconscious beliefs.

Know there are no right or wrong answers to the questions, only *your* answers. In addition to writing them down, I suggest answering them on a voice recorder such as the one on your smartphone. That allows you to listen to them while you're practicing Embodied Awareness. The more time you spend this way with the truth, the more comfortable you will become being in your body.

I found that listening to answers in my own voice is powerful, more powerful than reading them. Do both if you can.

Following TIME FOR YOUR TRUTH is a section titled SUGGESTED PRACTICE. The suggested practices will help you deepen your learning and forward your actions toward the specific intention identified through the questions.

Use Embodied Awareness when you read them to see if they feel right to you. When you do, other steps or practices may come to you that are better.

Challenge yourself to go beyond your comfort zone yet be gentle, too.

GROUNDING EXERCISE

Record this Grounding Exercise script and listen to it when you are ready.

- Sit comfortably with your feet on the ground.
- Close your eyes and inhale intentionally and deeply. Exhale and release all tension. Let your exhale be noisy if necessary. Repeat a few times until you feel more relaxed.
- Bring your awareness to your feet. Feel your feet on the ground. Know that under your feet, the earth is solid and supportive. Let your feet sink into the ground.
- Feel your body in your seat. Notice how you are sitting. Allow your seat to fully support you. Notice where your body touches the seat. There's nothing you need to do or fix. Just simply notice. Notice where your clothes touch your skin.
- Take an intentional inhale. Then take an intentional exhale.
- Notice whether or not you feel any air or breeze on your skin. Listen to the sounds in the environment. There may be layers of sound; simply notice them.
- Return your attention to the breath.
- Next, bring your awareness to your mouth. Notice how you are holding your jaw. Sense your tongue. There's no work for it to do. Open your lips slightly and relax your jaw. Breathe. Notice the wetness or dryness of your mouth and any tastes you sense.
- Bring your awareness to your nostrils. As you breathe, notice if you feel air on your nose. Feel your chest and abdomen rise and fall with each breath.
- With the next inhalation, follow your breath into your body. Breathe into the core of your being. Notice what's going on in your body. Simply notice.
- Spend a few breaths of awareness in your body.
- With your next inhalation, bring your awareness through your nasal passage as you follow the breath down through your neck.

- Let your awareness follow your breath into your chest and down deep into your abdomen.
- Keep going as you allow your awareness to flow through your legs and into your feet. Notice your feet solidly planted on the floor.
- Take one more cleansing inhale and exhale, then bring your awareness back into the room. Open your eyes.

Embodied Awareness

- Start with the Grounding Exercise. Next, answer, read, or listen to your responses to the questions in TIME FOR YOUR TRUTH. Notice what's happening in your body and the emotional energy that's present. Take time to just "be" with it. Instead of judging whatever you feel, welcome it like an old friend you love.
- If you notice any words or images or thoughts in Embodied Awareness, simply notice, take a breath, and put your awareness back into your body.
- When what you feel has stopped moving or tingling or existing, go on to the next question and answer and repeat.

Acknowledgment Cycle

In some of the Suggested Practices and elsewhere in this book, I speak to the Acknowledgment Cycle. When you practice the Acknowledgment Cycle, always start with the Grounding Exercise. Then after you feel grounded, practice Embodied Awareness.

Next, it's time to acknowledge what you are feeling and what you need, if anything. For example, you might bring to mind a situation that causes you to feel angry. It could involve a family member or friend, a work situation, a group you belong to, an activity, or something that only includes you. After you bring to mind the situation, "be" in that situation. Allow yourself to feel the emotions of that situation as if it were happening now.

Bring your awareness into your body. "Be" with what's happening within. Notice it. If words or stories or thoughts fill your mind, notice them and bring your awareness back to *what you feel* and *what is happening* inside your body.

Stay with this Embodied Awareness until you feel ready to inquire about what you need in this situation. What is your inner truth? What is your inner truth telling you? How can you give it to yourself? How might you love yourself more in this situation?

If you feel fear about what you know you need to do, start the Acknowledgment Cycle again and "be" with the energy of fear. Connecting with and acknowledging emotional energy allows it to transform and then lead into what you need.

Note: After practicing the Acknowledgment Cycle in the Suggested Practices and when you're alone, try it when you're actively engaged in a situation that's creating emotional energies. Trust yourself. Bring your awareness into your body. Without judgment or story, notice what's happening. Ask what you need in that moment. How can you honor yourself?

In the Beginning

Learning the Untruth

At three and a half years of age, I was accused of sexual misconduct.

This "indecent act" was carried out during a sunny play day in southern California while my cousin Steven and I were playing. Though playing together happened frequently, this day felt different to me. I was serious, focused, and intentional. Even at three and a half years, I somehow sensed this day would be important to the rest of my life.

We decided to play doctor although it was more than "just play" for me. I had a sense that my purpose was to be a healer—that I *was* a healer. Imagine! I hadn't even started nursery school yet.

That day, I took the role of the doctor and Steven was my patient. We found a make-do examination room in the back room of my family's house on 108th Street in Inglewood. This quiet room with white walls had the privacy of a doctor's office. Along the side of the wall separating the living room from our examination room was space on the floor where the doctor, me, could get to work.

"Theebon, way down pweese," I commanded Steven, my finger pointing to the examination table, which was an open space on the carpeted floor.

A good cousin and willing patient, Steven did as the doctor directed and plopped down on the carpet, his sun-bleached blond hair spread around his head. His arms flapped for a few seconds as he rubbed the soft beige carpet. When he stopped moving, his arms and body formed a "T" and his bare feet fell outward. I took a moment to observe him, yet I knew what to do. With the innocence of a three year old and the confidence of an old soul, I proceeded.

I grabbed the bottom of his t-shirt and struggled to pull it up tight under his armpits. He heaved his chest till his ribs pushed against his naked skin. His posture created space for his shirt to ease up along the floor. His tummy sloped down and disappeared into his shorts. My curiosity caused me to touch his belly button. He giggled.

A big moment was about to happen. I took a deep, doctor-like breath and looked at my patient's face before proceeding. With head tilted back and chin in the air, Steven's eyes explored the ceiling. I knelt down beside him and pressed my right ear to his skin just above where his bones poked out. My dark brown hair tickled his chest, and he giggled again.

"Theebon, sshhh! I'm gonna wissen to yoh hawt."

He became quiet. I squeezed my eyes shut and listened.

"What are you two doing? Lori, get off Steven! You are up to no good! You are bad! You should know better! Don't let me catch you doing that again!"

My father was really mad. His black eyebrows formed the letter V and his eyes looked scary. His lips smashed together each time he took a breath.

My shocked reaction poured forth in tears.

"Don't you cry or else I'll give you something to cry about! Get out of here! "he shouted.

The magic of listening to Steven's heart beating life into his little body was an opportunity never to happen. My broken heart beat faster than it ever had before. The innocence, the authentic intentions, the integrity of my little healer self were replaced with shame, guilt, and embarrassment.

"You're bad," he had shouted. And I took it in. I was bad; I was wrong; I shouldn't cry.

Fear fueled my legs as I ran away from the threat of my father.

What I Came to Know

The emotional trauma of being shamed for such an innocent intention seared a detailed memory in me forever. Only when I became a young adult did I understand that my father accused me of engaging in a sexual experience. I didn't know what sex was at that young age, but for sure I never played doctor again. And in an instant, I learned that being a healer was wrong.

Yet I knew, *really knew*, that being a healer was as true for me as the color of my hair is brown. I interpreted that early childhood experience as "there's something wrong about being my natural and true self."

From that moment on, I believed it was wrong to be me.

That marked the start of an ongoing training in which I was thoroughly and successfully taught that "who I was" was wrong, even unsafe, and that "what I felt" didn't matter. I learned that other people (especially men in power) were more important than me and that sex was repulsive.

As both a hypersensitive, intuitive child and old soul, I quickly understood that other people were *not* being their authentic selves either. Grownups seemed to live in a world they made up—one filled with lies, hurt, and blame. They also made up rules that didn't make sense to me. But since I had no voice or choice, I learned to play by the rules I was born into. *They* were right; *I* was wrong; the *untruth* was the truth.

Voices Taken Away

I have met many, too many, women whose voices and choices were also taken away from them. Like me, they were taught that they have less value than others, that what they feel is less important than others. They were also taught that the essence of their lives—their inner truth—is inconvenient, to be ignored, and flat-out wrong. This kind of conditioning occurs in our culture, in our religious institutions, and in our families. It's been happening for centuries.

Disassociating from our inner truth is a form of status quo in our society and part of mass (un)consciousness. Men learn it, too. We live this way until we've had enough or get so enraged or so depressed or so unhappy or victimized too many times that we're pushed to the tipping point of great change.

But I believe that with awareness, support, and courage, we can learn how to listen to our truth and give voice to it. Sadly, for some women including my mother and too many others, silence and oppression have followed them to the grave.

TIME FOR YOUR TRUTH

To start, practice at least one minute of grounding. (See Introduction for Grounding Exercise instructions.) Then ask the following questions one at a time. Be curious and gentle. After asking each question, close your eyes and *feel* into each answer.

Write down your answers and insights, taking special note of those that yield the strongest sensations in your body. I recommend answering them by speaking into a voice recorder on your smartphone or other device, then review them while practicing Embodied Awareness. (See Introduction for instructions on Embodied Awareness.)

Answer these questions:

1) What is your earliest positive childhood memory? What emotions does that memory hold?
2) What is your earliest negative childhood memory? What emotions does that memory hold?
3) What do you know that's true about you that you knew from an early age? How has that truth been accepted or judged by others? By you?
4) Be curious: What one experience in your childhood may have taught you an untruth about yourself?
5) What does *being authentic* mean to you?

SUGGESTED PRACTICE

Practice at least one minute of grounding and then take these actions:

- Take time this week to do something you loved doing as a child.
- Take time to acknowledge and honor a truth you've held since childhood—a truth born within you. Share that truth with someone you trust. Plan an activity that connects to that truth.
- Celebrate your truth!

The Truth about Anger

It's Not What You Think

Anger is a *natural human expression* and a *healthy emotional energy*—one that motivates change. As a powerful natural energy, anger helps us grow into our life's vision with integrity. It's like an organically self-generated truth serum that informs our every decision as we interact with our world and grow into our future.

Anger is a call to say "yes" to ourselves. Our inner truth of anger always has our back.

Anger has a biological component, too. Healthy emotional energy helps us as living organisms modulate behavior. That's scientific lingo for saying the healthy emotional energy of anger has helped our species survive and thrive.

A Living Organism

You may have the latest cut and color, volunteer at the local pet shelter, invest in your 401(k), attend the monthly book club, practice yoga, shop at TJ Max, and even channel an ascended master. Beneath all of those activities of the personality (the earthly home of your soul) is you, a living organism.

As a living organism, your anger provides an organic and appropriate response to your environment. If you let it, anger helps you adjust your behavior so you can survive *and* also thrive as an individual.

ANGER 101

Tapping into your anger helps you know what you need to have a fulfilling life as you accept the fullness of life.

But then you ask, "What about violence, abuse, rage? What about aggression, bullying, meanness?" Know this:

Anger is not violence. Violence is violence.

Anger is not abuse. Abuse is abuse.

Anger is not rage. Rage is rage.

Anger is not aggression. Aggression is aggression.

Anger is not about being a bully.

Anger is not about being mean.

We hear that people need anger management. But what they actually need is

- rage management
- violence management
- communication management
- honor your-true-feelings management

As a *healthy emotional energy,* anger doesn't need to be managed, so it shouldn't be lumped in with unhealthy reactions that differ from anger. Anger simply needs to be honored for the inner truth that it is. True anger doesn't complicate life; instead, it simplifies life.

Recognizing Anger

To honor anger for the inner truth that it is requires recognizing it. In turn, that requires self-awareness of our bodies. If we aren't grounded in our bodies, we are *not* aware of what's happening inside of us.

Our bodies create the healthy emotional energy of anger when we need information to respond authentically in the moment. Therefore, we can consider anger to be a sensation felt in the body without the labels, thoughts, and stories we attach to it. The healthy emotional energy of anger is not what we *think;* it's what we *feel.* Having an intellectual awareness of inner truth isn't enough.

Implementing the ideas in this book can help you better understand anger, but until you can *feel* your truth within your body, you won't be able to honor your inner truth, heed its wisdom, and create an authentic life.

How Anger Informs Us

Anger informs us with edicts such as these: "Based on what's going on in my life in this moment, somehow I need to love myself in a specific way. *I* need my attention. What specifically do I need right now? What do I need to say yes to? What do I need to say no to?"

We need not hunker down in a meditation position and ask the world to wait while we explore what's best for us (though this may be needed until we're adept at connecting to our inner truth). At times I still say, "Wait a minute. I need to connect with myself to see what I need."

Being in touch with anger requires awareness but not an intellectual capacity or logical understanding. Because I have a strong intellect, engaging my left brain sometimes serves me as long as I don't stay in my head.

For those of us who didn't or don't feel safe in our bodies, we tend to feel comfortable in our heads. I didn't feel safe in my body as a child so I developed a habit of thinking my way through life. As a result, I strengthened my mind. I can intellectualize and rationalize anything. The more I hear a new concept explained in different ways, the more my left brain relaxes, safe in its understanding. My rational mind can act like a security guard that won't let anything through the gate of my life castle unless it's fully convinced of its worthiness. Thus, my left brain is one tough cookie.

> *The more I understand a concept, the more easily I embody the concept and make it a living truth. But perhaps my left brain is saying that all too convincingly.*

Truth Resides in the Body

The thing is, inner truth doesn't reside in the head. In fact, being in our head can *prevent* us from getting in touch with our inner truth, which lives and moves through our body. This situation has been true for me.

If truth is only intellectualized, it will always be an effort. We can only *talk* our talk with intellectual understanding, but when we embody a truth, we can *walk* our talk. We can learn the steps of a dance but having to remember the steps and think about them while dancing takes effort. That effort gets in the way of dancing itself.

When we embody the dance, our cells remember the movements; we glide along the dance floor connected to the moment. That's when dancing becomes natural and intuitive; we *feel* the dance and we *are* the dance.

Similarly, when we embody a truth, we honor that truth organically without thinking about it. When we embody a truth, the left brain cannot argue with it, so it finds another battle to fight.

Now that I know what my anger feels like in my body and what it tells me, I don't need anger explained. However, because I've found a few explanations helpful over the years, I share them here.

The Five Elements

My first big insight about anger occurred when studying the Five Elements of Traditional Chinese Medicine, which are wood, fire, earth, air (or metal), and water. According to Chinese Medicine, we are part of the natural world. We too are made of these five elements, their interactions, and their dependencies with each other and our world. Each element is associated with a color, an emotion, a sound, a season, organs, officials, and meridians as well as how we interact with our environment. Each element has a purpose in nature. Knowing its purpose helps us see how the element is expressed in our own body and life.

The emotion of the wood element is anger. The sound of wood is shouting. The season is spring. The color is green. The officials are the gall bladder and liver officials. The officials do their work through the pathways of energy meridians.

To understand the expression of wood in our lives, picture a tree sapling in spring when the world is alive with green growth. As the sapling pushes out through the earth, it creates a new life, a new boundary, in a place none existed before the birth and growth.

The sapling claims its existence within the forest. "I am a tree!" Everything else in the forest is not the sapling tree. "You are not me!" it shouts. The sapling requires sunlight and nutrients and water from the soil. It needs to either protect itself from insects or attract them. Its boundary is sacred and, to survive and thrive as a living organism, that boundary must be maintained. The energy of anger helps maintain it.

A sapling tree will not say to another tree, "Okay, I need water but, hey, I'm not as important as you, so you take my share." No. It's survival. Its potential as a separate tree depends on honoring itself, giving itself what it requires. *There is no other way.*

The consciousness of all humanity is expressed through our separate identities, our separateness as individual living organisms, as it is for the sapling. Our boundary is our skin and the nerve endings in our skin that tell our brain "this is me" and "that is you." Without our boundary of skin, the mirror neurons in our brains wouldn't know the difference between *you being you* and *me being me.*

> *Our wood element helps us survive and thrive. It lets us know what we need so we can grow strong and into our full potential.*

Unlike a tree sapling, though, we can ignore our anger because with our cortex, we can even override the message of our wood element. If we ignore our anger enough times, our wood element becomes imbalanced and affects the other four elements. As humans, if we ignore our anger enough times, our lives won't feel fulfilling.

All the elements work together and influence each other. If your wood element is out of balance and you're not honoring your inner truth of anger, other parts of your life may get out of balance, too. Maybe you don't laugh as much as you'd like to (fire). Perhaps you yell a lot (wood). Maybe you're not nurturing yourself or you nurture others too much (earth). You may have low self-worth and cannot accept a compliment (air/metal). Perhaps you cry a lot and feel bitter about life (water). You may also develop an illness or disease from these imbalances.

Imbalances in the Elements

Imbalances in any of the other elements will also affect the wood element. As a living organism and energetic being, the fullness of your life is rich in relationship and connection—or lack thereof.

The officials doing the work of the wood element are the gall bladder and liver officials. The liver official helps with healthy body, mind, and spiritual growth. As the architect of life, it comes up with a plan to fulfill any vision we create.

Just like the seedling grows into a tree, the liver official helps us grow into our future. It's like the head honcho when it comes to our sense of direction. All other officials of all the other elements depend on our liver official. So if the liver official of the wood element—our anger—isn't being honored, our lives become imbalanced.

The gall bladder official is in charge of decisions and judgments. It helps us carry out the liver official's blueprint by making conscious decisions. In this way, the two officials work closely together. When our wood element is balanced and when we honor our anger, we create a blueprint for our life vision and make decisions that allow us to fulfill our vision.

My wood element was out of balance for years. I did not heed the inner voice of anger. I did not honor my boundaries. Instead, I poured my life force into other people's visions and blueprints, and I neglected to do the same for me.

Our wood element wants us to consult our vision at every occasion, but for me, my vision wasn't even a part of the conversation. Feeling unfulfilled and resentful, I felt burdened by obligation. Any simplicity eluded me. As a tree sapling, I remained dwarfed and deficient.

Today, my life is mostly in balance. Still, when I see an acupuncturist, I learn it's still the wood element that needs most attention.

Role of Core Values

My professional coach training taught me the fundamental importance of having core values in our lives. Core values are areas we hold in high regard. When our behaviors and decisions align with our core values, life is simpler and more fulfilling. When we do not honor our core values, our decisions don't reflect what's important to us. That's when we feel unfulfilled, frustrated, and resentful. If we can't name what we value, then we're out of touch with what's important to us.

Said another way, when our choices don't align with our core values, we can feel a deep dissatisfaction within. Unless we connect with that dissatisfaction and listen to its wisdom, we will continue to ignore what's truly important to us. More than that, our inner voice of anger will build an increasing inner pressure that seeks release.

The best way to release the pressure is to say "yes" to ourselves in a conscious way; however, if we continue to ignore the healthy emotional energy of anger, the pressure explodes in a way that doesn't honor inner truth or feel good. That pressure can explode *outwardly* and hurt others or ourselves. Or it can explode *inwardly* and cause excess stress, unhappiness, and illness. Or both.

When your choices don't reflect what's important to you *and* you're disconnected from the inner truth of anger, you create inner conflict. Here's an example.

You say your top three core values are 1) spending time with family, 2) good health, eating right, and exercising, and 3) being in nature. But you work ten hours a day and you constantly volunteer for service opportunities, eat junk food, and never take a walk in the park. Without doubt, you'll find your life fulfillment lacking.

This observation may be obvious, but it's uncanny how many people make choices that aren't aligned with what they value. I was one of them.

The Boyfriend and Buddy

By the time I graduated from high school, I was deeply unhappy. I wasn't thriving. I didn't know what my core values were. I didn't know what inner truth was. I had no boundaries. I ignored my anger. I didn't value myself. I had no sense of self or self-worth. I had no worthy male role models in my childhood. My life was a perfect recipe to create suffering. And suffer I did.

By the time I met Craig, who became my boyfriend, I was deeply unhappy. It's ironic to apply the "friend" part to him because he mentally and physically abused me for most of our years together.

Craig and I lived in a shabby historic wooden cottage situated along a country back road near Palmyra, Pennsylvania. From the outside, it looked like a storybook house, but on the inside, life was difficult. The cottage had broken windows, no furniture except for a bed and a kitchen table, and no insulation. Using an old oil hot water baseboard heater cost us a fortune in the winter for heating—money we didn't have.

Within the first year of living there, we knew we needed a new place that was winterized and more affordable. While looking for a rental, my boyfriend said he wanted a dog—specifically, a pedigreed Russian Wolfhound puppy. He knew someone who had a litter of pups about an hour away, but we needed to go see them right away if we were interested.

I disagreed with his surprising idea of getting a puppy. Even back then, a puppy like that cost several hundred dollars to buy. How could we afford it? Plus looking for a rental that would accept a dog would be difficult. On top of all that, in conservative Lancaster County, landlords generally didn't rent to unmarried couples. I was already scared we wouldn't find a place and didn't need another strike against us. So I voiced my concerns to Craig and suggested we not get a dog.

But expressing my concern invited physical abuse. Suddenly, Craig would let nothing get in the way of his mission to get a puppy. He forced me into the car and threw me in the front seat. He pulled out of the driveway and started speeding down the 25 mph back road at about 50 mph.

"Craig, please slow down! I'm scared!"

With that, he stepped on the gas pedal and drove even faster. Then with his left hand on the steering wheel, he swung his right arm and fist, and punched my face and body intermittently for the hour-long drive. I could almost hear my father's harsh voice in this experience: "Don't cry, Lori, or I'll give you something to cry about."

We arrived at the puppy house in York about one hour later. I was well-trained by then so I didn't dare try to run away, but just in case, he wasn't going to let anything interfere with getting a puppy.

"You're going in with me," Craig declared and made me get out of the car.

We walked up to the front porch, and he knocked on the door. I stood in the shadow, silent trying not to cry or look like a woman who had just been beaten for an entire hour. I felt ashamed. My face must have been red and swollen, but when the woman of the house answered the door, she didn't seem to notice. I forced a smile.

It's interesting how so many of us will avoid the obvious: the truth. I avoided being truthful with others and myself about the horror of my life, and a stranger with puppies avoided the obvious presence of an abused woman on her front porch.

With this truth successfully ignored, Craig pushed me to go in first. The woman who answered the door and other family members formed a circle around the cute Russian Wolfhound puppies. They were cooing and petting them as they told us the personality traits and show dog qualities for each puppy. I looked on in shock while Craig petted them. He made his decision quickly. We went home with Buddy.

Of course, I fell in love with Buddy. That was fortunate, too, because the way it turned out, I was forced to look after him. Craig's desire for a puppy didn't include caring for one, so I cleaned up puppy poop in the house, walked him, fed him, washed him, and brushed him.

Buddy was beautiful and soft but not very trainable. When he got loose, he ran as fast as the wind until he became a dot on the horizon. Still, Buddy kept me company when I was lonely. He became my teddy bear when I needed a hug. And I needed a hug often.

Mostly, Buddy taught me about loyalty. The loyalty I had learned as a child was not an honorable kind of loyalty. I was devoted to men in my life who had not earned it. I'd learned that other people, especially men in power, were more important than me because *I didn't matter*. My life was all about them, not me.

Apparently, I was more trainable than Buddy. For all of his foibles, he was true to the dog he was. Buddy had instincts he couldn't override no matter how much I tried to train him. He ran fast at every opportunity; he chased any creature he could; he protected his pack mate—me. Yes, I had earned Buddy's loyalty.

A Day of Rage

One day (as on many other days), Craig became intense and full of rage. As usual, I was to blame for something. He sneered his complaint at me as I sat on the sofa in the corner of the living room. Then he approached

ANGER 101

me with that "look." I went from watching TV to defending myself by raising my hands to protect my face.

For him, hitting me escalated into a whole new expression of rage. That day, Craig used the weight of his body to push me down along the length of the sofa, then he wrapped his hands around my neck and started to choke me. I tried to pull his hands off while my crying voice scratched out "Craig, stop! Please stop."

Though my pleas never worked, I tried them anyway. And my usual pattern included defending my actions since I hadn't done what he accused me of doing. But my defense of the truth never worked, for no one can reason with rage.

Craig's body bore down on me with a lifetime of pent-up energy created long before he met me. Likewise, I received his abuse with a body that had taken on a lifetime of being victimized. We were puzzle pieces that fit together: two unaware people who continued a pattern of untruth and drama learned as children.

My clenched screams sounded an alarm for the only other living being in the house. A growling Buddy ran into the living room and jumped on Craig's back. Docile, untrained Buddy was fierce and frantic at seeing me being violated. When he sunk his teeth into Craig's leg and pulled, Craig was forced to release his hold on me. I rolled out from underneath him and ran out of the house. Buddy's protecting me released me from the moment's violence, but he became the next victim to be beaten. And there was nothing I could do to stop it.

Buddy was *loyal* to me in a way I could not be for myself. He *protected* me in a way I could not protect myself. He *valued* me in a way I did not value myself. He *showed* me I was worth fighting for.

The day I finally moved out of the house, I left Buddy behind. I didn't know where I was going, but I knew he couldn't go with me. I had to learn to take care of myself first. Yet Buddy had taught me I was too important to be loyal to others at the expense of my own precious life. This beloved dog that I didn't want, that I had raised, and that saved my life had to remain with the man who purchased him.

Trauma as a Catalyst for Change

After leaving Craig, I was never again in an abusive relationship; however, I still prioritized the needs of others over my own. When I reached my early thirties, I started to learn how to say "yes" to myself more and more. At that time, the way for me to learn to honor my inner truth—as is often true for most people—was more trauma. Trauma becomes the catalyst for change.

Choosing unconditional self-love, the ultimate "yes" for ourselves, doesn't require trauma to inspire it. We simply need to *acknowledge* our inner truth in the moment and then *honor* ourselves by loving ourselves. The process of acknowledgment and honor needs conscious practice until it becomes a habit. But until we learn of another way to live and learn, trauma remains our teacher.

Nowadays, listening to my inner truth of anger is a habit, a healthy habit. It informs me about the moment and what's best for me, even if it is just a polite "no thank you." I love myself now without having to be traumatized and yet, big life events can still move me closer to the truth more quickly, deeply, and purely than gentle nudges.

> *The blessing of my experiences and training is that I help people connect with their inner truth without having to go through trauma. I teach them how to use their power consciously.*

Ignoring Your Inner Truth

So how do you know when you're ignoring your inner truth of anger? Could it be when the outside of you is in conflict? Or when your life is not fulfilling? Perhaps when you are exhausted at making an effort to improve your life, but it doesn't get better.

Are you ignoring your inner truth when everyone seems to be more important than you? For sure, if you're a victim of repeated abuse as I was, you're certainly ignoring your inner truth—and if that's true, I implore you to leave that environment right away.

The first time I *felt* the healthy emotional energy of anger with Craig was on our first date. The first time I *ignored* my healthy emotional anger with Craig was on our first date. The first time my inner truth told me that *I should not be with Craig* was on our first date—and every moment thereafter for several years.

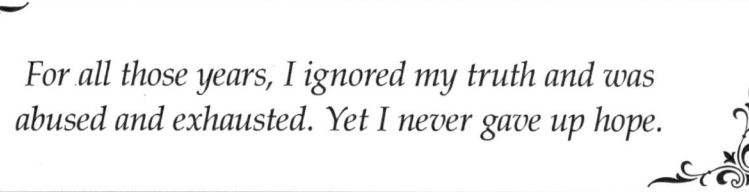

For all those years, I ignored my truth and was abused and exhausted. Yet I never gave up hope.

Yes, the effort of keeping the untruth alive is exhausting. It takes a lot of energy and effort to keep our inner truth suppressed. As powerful beings, we can use our power in any way we consciously or unconsciously choose. Indeed, every choice we make is an expression of our power.

I suggest you look within to find your answers and then allow that inner wisdom to lead you to consciously choose how to use your power. When you get good at being connected to your inner truth of anger, disempowered choices are no longer part of your life. And then the energy required to keep inner truth suppressed is released, transformed, and available to honor your life in new, authentic ways.

Anger is an invitation to self-loving. It's wise, loving, and honorable; it's an organic, natural, and authentic response. Anger is "me-ness" and not "meanness."

Your success in life depends on keeping your inner truth as a priority and never giving somebody else's needs or wants precedence over yours. Therefore, you must be your own advocate of inner truth; no one can do that for you. Someone might coach you on inner truth, speak about it, and write about it. But only *you* as an individual have the power to choose inner truth above all else—and live life authentically.

TIME FOR YOUR TRUTH

To start, practice at least one minute of grounding. (See Introduction for instructions.)

Then ask the following questions one at a time. Be curious and be gentle. After asking each question, close your eyes and *feel* into each answer.

Write down your answers and insights, taking special note of those that yield the strongest sensations in your body. I recommend answering them by speaking into a voice recorder on your smartphone or other device. Then review them while practicing Embodied Awareness. (See Introduction for instructions.)

1) What is your perception of anger?
2) What are your top five core values? What core values do you regularly honor? What core values do you regularly ignore?
3) When do you feel *disempowered* and what is your role in that experience? When do you feel *empowered* and what is your role in that experience?
4) What does empowerment feel like in your body?
5) When do you prioritize the needs of others over your own needs? How often is this experience an unconscious habit, a fear-based

choice, a compulsion, a conscious choice, or something else? As you reflect on it, how does each instance feel?

SUGGESTED PRACTICE

Again, practice at least one minute of grounding and then take these actions:

- Choose a core value that needs your attention and commit to honoring it this week.
- After honoring your chosen core value, record how the commitment and action felt to you. Practice Embodied Awareness. Use words that represent how your body felt and specifically the sensations in the body. For example, you might say, "My chest felt lighter; my smile was so wide it stretched my face; my legs wanted to jump up and down," and so on.
- Celebrate your commitment to yourself.

On Being a Bitch

Bitches Are Not Beige

I'm a bitch. Based on the title of this book, being a bitch is a healthy aspiration. Of course, that's my opinion, and an opinion that I value above all others. After decades of not having an opinion or valuing myself, this idea is one I can firmly stand on.

I know being a bitch has a bad rap, just like anger. Simply being *me* had a bad rap for most of my life. But here's the thing: *Bad raps are not the truth.* Only truth is the truth. And bitches in America have been getting a bad rap for over 150 years. That's how long a large enough majority of women in America has been speaking the truth and acting on it.

But I'm done with the bad rap. Instead, I'm all about embodying and honoring truth as I experience it *when* I experience it.

Through *Anger 101* and in my work, I intend to shift the perception of anger and being a bitch in a positive, life-affirming way. The new perception: "The healthy approach to being a bitch" embodies the healthy, emotional energy of anger.

That intention for me goes hand in hand with my changing perception about who I am and who I am not. It's all based on my inner truth, which I uncover more and more each day. Writing this book has helped me continue to unlearn the untruth about me, and if I can help others in the process, that's wonderful.

ANGER 101

Create New Rules

I know far too many women who give their whole lives away based on the untruth and oppressive rules taught to them by others. Yet we have the choice to create new rules.

> *Bitches are great at creating new rules. And bitches are great at changing things for the better.*

The healthy approach to being a bitch is *not* based on the definition of bitch from Webster's New World College Dictionary, Fourth Edition.

bitch (bich) *n.* 1 the female of the dog, wolf, fox, etc.; 2 [Archaic] a lewd or promiscuous woman; a malicious, bad-tempered, or aggressive woman; 3 [Slang] anything especially unpleasant or difficult; 4 [Slang] a complaint.

I aspire to live up to the definition of bitch based on how I perceive American history. Admittedly, even if the history of bitches (as I understand it) isn't true, my history of not honoring my inner truth *is* true. Either way, I stand on the following claim: *There is a healthy approach to being a bitch, which is achieved by honoring the inner voice of anger.*

History's Lesson

In the years leading up to the 1840s, American women were growing weary of the injustices they experienced. In 1848, a formalized movement began in Seneca Falls, New York, with the first women's rights convention. The leaders of the Seneca Falls meeting, Elizabeth Cady Stanton and Lucretia Mott, along with hundreds of others started the campaign that would carry on for almost three quarters of a century.

That campaign resulted in the 19th Amendment that gave women in the U.S. the right to vote.

Although gaining women the vote was perhaps the most radical demand at the time, it was not their only concern. The women in the suffragette movement were angry about the many injustices against girls and women in America.

For those of us living in 2016—the year that saw Hillary Clinton be the first woman to run for a major party in a presidential election—it may seem surprising to know this: Only 100 years earlier, in the century I was born, women had fewer constitutional rights than men to participate in the laws of the land, their households, and even their own personal lives (and bodies). That included both white men and former male slaves.

Girls did not have equal educational opportunities as most colleges and universitites were closed to women. In some states, girls as young as 10 years old could be married. Women did not have control over their bodies. With childbearing regarded as a duty, motherhood was not voluntary, and a woman's body legally belonged to her husband.

Women and girls were not protected under law from drunken and abusive fathers. In some cases, women couldn't testify against their husbands because it was illegal to do so.

In contrast, husbands had rights to their wives' money and property while a wife had no such rights. Fathers had automatic court-imposed child custody rights; mothers did not. Men could marry a foreign national and retain American citizenship, but women who married a foreign national lost it.

Free speech in America wasn't free for women. It was even common that women couldn't pray out loud in church. The suffragettes generally shared the conviction, which was evidenced by everyday experiences, that the government and church supported the oppression of women.

The women who gathered in 1848—including other suffragette leaders such as Susan B Anthony, Lucy Stone, and Frances Willard—used their voices, their ability to write, travel, and petition to change the status quo. These courageous woman raised money for their cause and earned income, however low it was, to carry their campaign onward. They traveled to state after state throughout North America during a time when travel wasn't simple. Though some were married to men, all were married to the pursuit of liberty.

For 72 years, from 1848 to 1920, in the face of harsh and at times tortuous oppression and criticism, the American suffragettes persisted with their peaceful campaigns. As these women became more public with their opinions, voices, and campaigns of change, so did their critics and oppressors. The American suffragettes' peaceful means did not prevent their brutal arrests or torture by those who oppressed them.

These suffragettes were visionaries. They knew that even if they didn't achieve the right to vote in their lifetimes, women who came after them eventually would. Long after many of the original leaders in the suffragette movement had died, the 19th Amendment was ratified in 1920.

Around 1920 and the years following, the word "bitch" as a deragotory term for women rose in usage. "Bitch" was used to label outspoken women—those considered contemptible, malicious, and mean.

Yet, what we know is this: These first American bitches were not contemptible, malicious, or mean. They were heroic, honorable, and powerful. Their anger was not only healthy; it was appropriate and peaceful.

 *Their anger became the energy of change.*

A New Definition

These first American "bitches" changed American history and the world in a positive, life-affirming way. And they did it through relentless, non-violent constitutional methods.

There's nothing about being a real bitch, therefore, that deserves a bad rap. Perhaps the definition from Webster about bitches being "unpleasant and difficult" rings true when stretching it a bit. Certainly the difficult work to make the 19th Amendment law was unpleasant. This honorable change to society was surely unsettling to the status quo of the era.

In truth, aspiring to be a bitch means aspiring to be heroic, honorable, and powerful. It requires listening to the inner voice of anger and heeding its wisdom.

Thus, based on my interpretation of history, my new definition for the word bitch becomes:

bitch (bich) *n.* 1 the female of the dog, wolf, fox, etc.; 2 a) a heroic, honorable, and powerful woman, b) a woman connected to her inner truth of anger, c) a woman who intentionally creates change by honoring the healthy emotional energy of anger.

Imagine if anger were honored in our world and more women were worthy of being bitches. If that were true, *there would be more harmony.* And I'm not joking; I sincerely believe that. Bitches have more in common with saints than they do with the devil. I certainly don't need

ANGER 101

to be a saint and I don't believe in the devil, but I *am* finished with being the doormat, pushover, and victim.

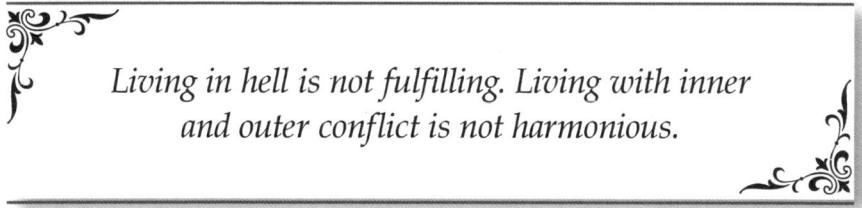

Living in hell is not fulfilling. Living with inner and outer conflict is not harmonious.

Personal Origins

When my grandmothers were born, the term "bitch" was used as the proper description for female dogs. My German American grandmother Amelia Yoder, nee Machamer, had most likely heard and used the term as she was raised on a farm.

My Italian American grandmother Rose DiGuardi, nee Rossi, probably rarely heard the term. Grandmom DiGuardi, who lived her whole life in the city, probably didn't have reason to talk about dogs. Aunt Millie, Grandmom's daughter who's in her mid-90s, said there was much discussion about the mean Italian women in the city. When the Italian women who were perceived as "mean" walked down the street, people crossed to the other side. These mean women weren't called bitches; they were called Sicilians.

That story makes me want to defend Sicilians, especially after spending three weeks in Sicily a few years ago. I didn't meet any women who made me want to cross the street and walk on the other side. In fact, the opposite was true.

Sicilian Sisters

On that trip, I met two beautiful Sicilian sisters who were both at one time unhappily married. They both decided to end their marriages, leave their husbands, and get divorced. As a result, the two women faced relentless backlash from people in their conservative Catholic small-island culture and medieval village. Rather than follow traditions that didn't honor their truths, they found the courage to live in emotional integrity. They chose to create lives more meaningful to them as women rather than be blindly loyal to their former husbands, outdated traditions, or "men in authority positions."

During a drive to a family picnic at the base of Mt. Etna, the sisters told me of the death of their beloved aunt. Neither sisters spoke English nor was my Italian up to par, so the story was translated by my new friend and their cousin, Vincent, who sat in the back seat with me.

When their aunt died, her husband refused to hold a wake for her. It wasn't important to him to dress her in a beautiful outfit for burial or do her hair or makeup. So the sisters' inner truth of anger motivated them to honor their aunt in a way she deserved. During an opportune moment, they kidnapped their aunt's body. It may seem as if they stole a dead body, but instead they lovingly embraced and consecrated their aunt's death in a way this woman deserved.

In effect, they graced their aunt's death with love. They dressed her in a beautiful new dress, fixed her hair, and made up her face. Then they held a memorial in her honor. After they honored their beloved aunt, they released her body to the husband so he could bury her.

Listening to the stories of these two women, I was in awe of the commitment they'd shown to their inner truth, to love, and to honor. They earned my respect and admiration. Could I ever be as courageous as they were? I was happy to walk on any street with them.

> *Many called them "bitches" in a derogatory way. But for me, they are true to the definition of bitch as I define it—heroic, honorable, and powerful.*

Changing the Status Quo

When we listen to our voice of anger and make conscious choices informed by that anger, we upset the status quo. That comes with growing pains, for there will always be people who don't like our choices. Our relationships will change. Even when we give ourselves permission to show up more authentically, we will feel uncomfortable for a while. We're experiencing the death of an outdated "self" and that's a loss. And when we expand our comfort zones, we often experience fear of our unknown. But we also find a more truthful future.

However, any discomfort will be temporary. Growing into our future with our inner truth leading the way is as natural as any process can be. And it's a main reason our souls incarnate as humans.

As we experience the discomfort of conscious choice, our souls and inner selves celebrate with joy. Growing into our vision and toward the light is heroic, honorable, and powerful. When listening to our inner truth becomes an expanded *new* status quo, we know we are creating our most fulfilling life.

Still Targeted Today

Since the enactment of the 19th Amendment and still today, women who stand up for equality continue to be targeted with unfavorable words. We women are far stronger than those whose mouths are the harbingers for fear of change.

I remember in 2012 when Georgetown University student Sandra Fluke testified to a congressional committee about birth control. Her manner was respectful, clear, and mature, and her well-expressed truth represented the experience of many female college students in America. The only female to testify to a panel of all men in power, she was heroic and honorable. Her willingness to speak up was powerful.

A few days later, though, Sandra was called a slut and prostitute on the national airwaves because she dared to speak up for women's right to birth control.

Women still suffer the wrath of those who like to keep things the same. People who fear change or powerful women try to force them into subjugated positions through derogatory labels, harassment, violence, and traditional and religious beliefs. Although equality for the sexes is growing, not all women in America have equality and certainly not all women around the world. Our culture still unconsciously supports collective beliefs about how women should behave and the roles they should play. It's still unconscious in its reactions when women challenge the status quo. It's not only men who fear powerful women; women fear their own power, too. In many parts of the world, a woman doesn't have to be powerful to be murdered. Simply being female is enough.

Genocide Resides in Everyday News

This female genocide resides in our shared history as well as in everyday news. Women have been murdered, executed, tortured, raped, abused, and violated for centuries. So many women of today are still afraid of their power, their truth, their expression of making a difference.

In America, several of my female friends are afraid to practice their healing modalities or psychic abilities because of our shared collective past of female healers being killed during the Middle Ages. I have also shared this fear for my own intuitive healing abilities.

This tells me our collective history is alive and yet, as more of us connect with and honor our truth, we create a new paradigm in which women and men embody their authentic power. This is good for all humanity.

> *When we embody heroism, honor, and authentic power, we shift the consciousness of our shared history, heal the karma of our ancestors, and create a more peaceful future for everyone.*

Teaching Her to Be Beige

In a speech at the National Cathedral, Marianne Williamson spoke about the female genocide of the Middle Ages. I could feel the truth embedded in her words about the consciousness of that time. She said, "If every passionate free-thinking female is marched off, God forbid, to the stake to be burned, after enough centuries, if you have a little girl with sparkle, you teach her to be beige."

Fear is the force that fuels genocide. And oppression. That fear makes humans want power over others. One way to win the power struggle is by murdering and oppressing those you fear. History records the number of women killed during the Middle Ages to be from tens of thousands to millions of women. Bless their souls. For all the women who were marched off to meet their death in the fiery hell created by the early church and government of the time, anger was an appropriate response. But these women were not called bitches; they were called witches.

Our history and global consciousness still oppress women. That's why we women must be all the more gentle and loving toward ourselves, our truth, and each other. To create change in our own lives and in our world, we must be heroic, honorable, and powerful. Indeed, we must be the change we want to see in our world. The time for being beige is over.

My Work in Uganda

I learned how to be less beige with my work in Uganda. As a white woman in Africa, I was prepared to stick out no matter what. Many people in the capital of Kampala and the village of Kyanja depended on me to provide fundamental needs as well as raise standards through my work with Brain Tree Primary School, a school for underprivileged children and orphans.

Working for and with Brain Tree, I raised money, oversaw capital projects, and provided accountability. My responsibility forced me to have a voice, to be visible and accountable in a way that required me to be heroic, honorable, and powerful for children.

Over fifteen years, I traveled to Uganda several times. Compared to life in America—even compared to my early life as a welfare child and then an abused woman—everyday life in Uganda was an immense struggle, a life of survival.

For women, life is even tougher than for men. Women don't have many rights in Uganda; I'm not sure if they have *any*. My Ugandan female friends have told me they learned to say "no" to others only after living in America. Corruption, poverty, and a semi-police state keep people struggling to survive and afraid to speak up. Those who questioned authority or another's integrity could easily have their lives or livelihoods threatened.

During those years, I became a voice for a school, for children, and at times for a village. I would learn to question the integrity of others.

A Library for Brain Tree

In 2006, we built a library for Brain Tree and filled it with books. At the time, it was one of our biggest projects in the history of the school. As the construction of the library was carried out in Kyanja, I started collecting over 5,000 books at my house in Pennsylvania. I reviewed each of the 5,000 books one by one and chose 2,500 books most appropriate for a Ugandan primary school. Under the skilled tutelage of librarians in my children's school, volunteers manually catalogued the books. Cataloging entails looking at each book, writing down its data, giving it a spine label with a Dewey Decimal number, and placing a book pocket and book card inside the back cover. It was a lot of work.

After cataloging, the books were packed into forty-two boxes equaling two cubic meters. Each box was taped and shipping labels affixed on three sides. My Ugandan brother Lutwama rented a truck that we loaded with the book boxes. Lutwama drove the books to Boston. From there, the freight was put in a container to be placed on a ship. And away it cruised on the high seas for two months heading to Kenya.

Once the shipment arrived in Kenya, it was loaded onto a truck and driven west across the country to Kampala, Uganda. In Kampala, the books went through customs and clearing. After that step, the local shipping agent, Mr. Kiwanaka, picked up the forty-two book boxes. He was supposed to call the leaders of Brain Tree to arrange delivery, and the ETA of those boxes would be between the end of April and mid-May.

However, I got to Uganda in mid-June and the books had not arrived yet. The local shipping agent kept saying to the school directors "tomorrow" but tomorrow the books never came. This went on for over a month. We had planned a library grand opening for the entire community on July 3rd and we needed the library to be complete.

I find it easy to be heroic, honorable, and powerful on behalf of children. And in my years of my working with Brain Tree, I got a lot of practice.

With the grand opening of the library just a few weeks away, no books, and only empty promises from the shipping agent, it was time to ruffle the status quo. I called the Ugandan shipper in America and told him we hadn't received the books. That call resulted in us hearing from Mr. Kiwanaka. Again, he made a promise to deliver the books "tomorrow," which would be Friday afternoon.

At noon on Friday, a large van pulled up to the front of the school, the books finally being delivered. The entire school of about a hundred and fifty children and a dozen teachers surrounded Mr. Kiwanaka and his van. We opened the back doors to see inside—the book boxes that had traveled half way around the world.

Several bigger children start unloading the boxes immediately while the other children sang, clapped, and danced. How exciting! The Brain Tree students—ever obedient and overly eager to please me—carried the boxes toward the new library.

"Please stop! We need to count how many boxes have arrived. Please place them here," I shouted.

I pointed to the ground behind the open doors of the van. Too much effort went into preparing the books and building the library for even one book to be missing. And with corruption in Uganda, you never know when people think they need your stuff more than you do.

After all the book boxes were placed on the ground, the entire school community counted the number of boxes together. Thirty-nine. I took a deep breath and looked at Mr. Kiwanaka.

"Three boxes are missing," I informed him.

"I'll go back to the warehouse and find the missing boxes," he replied.

"When?" I asked.

ANGER 101

"This afternoon."

To me, that sounded a lot like "tomorrow." I knew the entire school depended on me to make things happen—to be heroic, honorable, and powerful for them. I could sense it from the crowd. I could feel that in myself.

All the children and teachers looked at me as I looked at Mr. Kiwanaka. What do I do? This was no time to be beige.

"Everyone, please look at Mr. Kiwanaka." Heads turned. At least one hundred seventy pairs of eyes focused on him. My thoughts raced. I knew we had a library to complete, and I was expecting to do business respectfully. I normally don't make a fuss in Uganda. Knowing everything is more challenging there than in America, I tend to go with the Ugandan flow.

However, this time, I wasn't willing to surrender my emotional integrity to someone who seemed comfortable operating in a corrupt culture. I felt my chest fill with a sensation that prodded me to speak up. I felt anger. I was motivated to do things right.

"Mr. Kiwanaka, I would like you to give us your word that you will find those boxes and deliver them to us this afternoon. You wouldn't want to disappoint a whole school of children, would you?"

Mr. Kiwanaka's eyebrows climbed up his forehead. I, too, was surprised at my forthrightness. But my eyes remained glued to Mr. Kiwanaka, and we waited a long time for his answer. His face relaxed as he found his voice. "I will return as promised."

I turned and looked at the schoolyard of eyes, then I echoed his pledge to the school. "Mr. Kiwanaka says he will return with the three boxes of books this afternoon. Does everyone understand what Mr. Kiwanaka has promised us?"

"Yes" was the resounding reply.

I felt a bit like a crazy women at our discourse, but later, when Mr. Kiwanaka kept his promise and delivered the three remaining boxes, I felt vindicated. Upon his return, he said he couldn't disappoint so many children.

My business with Mr. Kiwanaka was not finished, though. He handed me his invoice for payment. I saw he charged us far more than the shipper in America quoted—another common practice in a culture that sometimes lacks integrity and good business practices.

I looked over the costs and asked him to explain various unfamiliar line items. Rather than answer the question, he surprised me by saying, "Well, we can cross that one off. This one, too." (Invalid costs have no explanation, apparently.) After marking each questioned amount with a big X, his remaining cost was close to the estimate quoted.

On the day of its grand opening two weeks later, our library was complete and beautiful—totally worth all the effort.

Working for the children in Uganda gave me fifteen years of practice standing up for the truth. In a land of survival, there's no time to buy into my personal false beliefs. Being present in the moment and listening to my inner truth was the only way I could create the change these children needed for their fundamental needs.

> *This work taught me how to connect to my inner truth for others. Yet it was still more difficult to be consistently heroic, honorable, and powerful for me.*

A Deep Hunger

When we aren't connected to our inner truth, we will find other people, places, and things that highlight what we're denying in our own selves. The children of Uganda touched upon a deep hunger in me to love children and support them no matter what. That need mirrored my own need to love and support myself *no matter what*. It was the need for love and support missing during my childhood. I had no idea then how my silent hunger had become a compelling force.

When we aren't connected to our inner truth and therefore our inner needs, often we feel compelled to help others, fix others, and give them what we think they need. We see in them what we're denying in ourselves.

But when we're aligned with our inner truth, we are less compelled to do for others. Instead, we're more apt to make a conscious choice to help them *because we are already honoring our own needs*. We are better able to make choices from fullness and not from lack.

Being a bitch means being heroic, honorable, and powerful for ourselves and others because, given my definition, *a bitch is woman who's connected to her inner truth of anger.*

> *A bitch loves herself and is guided by her inner wisdom. She serves herself first because she knows that emotional integrity is required for authentic power. And authentic power is required for sustained and empowered change.*

TIME FOR YOUR TRUTH

To start, practice at least one minute of grounding. (See Introduction for Grounding Exercise instructions.) Then ask the following questions one at a time. Be curious and be gentle. After asking each question, close your eyes and *feel* into each answer.

Write down your answers and insights, taking special note of those that yield the strongest sensations in your body. I recommend answering them by speaking into a voice recorder on your smartphone or other device. You would review them while practicing Embodied Awareness. (See Introduction for instructions on Embodied Awareness.)

1) How often do you use the word bitch? What meaning do you give it?
2) Have you ever been called a bitch? Why?
3) Have you ever called another woman a bitch in a derogatory way? What was your reason?
4) Where in your life *would you like to be* heroic, honorable, and powerful for yourself? What is possible when you are heroic, honorable, and powerful for yourself?
5) Where in your life *have you been* heroic, honorable, and powerful for yourself? How did that feel?
6) Are there times you feel compelled to help other people who haven't asked for help? Describe those people and their needs. How might that be a reflection of how you need to show up for yourself?

SUGGESTED PRACTICE

Again, practice at least one minute of grounding and then take these actions:

- Choose an area of your life that is asking you to be heroic, honorable, and powerful for yourself. Practice the Acknowledgment Cycle (see instructions in the Introduction). Take inspired action for that area. It can be as simple as taking fifteen minutes to soak in the bath when others are asking for your time and attention, or telling your friends or neighbors how you feel about their behavior. You'll know right away what needs your attention, so please be gentle with yourself and don't talk yourself out of your truth.
- After completing your inspired action, write down or record how you feel.
- Celebrate honoring your truth!

Living the Lie

Disassociation with Inner Truth

Living life in a way that disregards the inner truth comes about through many experiences. Here, I share events that shaped my life as a woman, mother, professional, and personal development coach. By no means do my examples provide a complete explanation of why and how we grow into the humans we become. But what I share has helped me and those I have served.

As soon as we are born, we have full time jobs. One is growing our physical bodies into adulthood; the other is learning what life is all about. As we grow and learn, we depend on our caregivers to provide the fundamentals of life so we can survive and thrive. We look to them for our basic needs as well as to acknowledge who we are. In return, we get the rules of life that our caregivers follow as they consciously and unconsciously create a life for themselves and for us.

We are born embodying our truth—we *are* our truth—but aren't yet able to express it. As souls, we may have chosen our place and family of origin, but as soon as we slide through the birth canal and take our first independent breath, we start growing up with the constraints or freedoms we're born into. From there starts the learning of the untruth.

Sometimes our life lessons support the truth we're born with. Often, though, what we learn in childhood negates our truth.

> *Our early years become a roadmap of beliefs we follow as we navigate our lives—for better or worse.*

Is What We Feel Correct?

From childhood, we're taught that almost everyone and everything is more of an expert on us than we are of ourselves. Our caregivers keep us alive; they feed us, keep us safe, and if we are fortunate, they love us—and sometimes they teach us that what we feel is not correct. *We must be wrong.* The teaching can be (and often is) innocent. Either way, it's impossible to not be influenced by the beliefs of others or the culture we're born into. There's no escaping it; this is life on earth.

Take for instance the following example dialogs:

Child: "I'm tired."
Adult: "You can't be tired. You just slept for eight hours!"

Child: "I'm hungry!"
Adult: "No you aren't! You just ate lunch."

Child: "It's cold in here."
Adult: "You are crazy. I'm sweating!"

Child: "That music is giving me a headache. Can you turn it down?"
Adult: "I can hardly hear it. You are just trying to annoy me."

Child: "I can't concentrate. I can't do this homework right now."
Adult: "You just want to play and get out of doing your work."

~

Child: "I don't like the way this tastes."
Adult: "Eat it right now or you don't get dessert."

~

Child: "I'm upset that Mary took my toys."
Adult: "Play nice or you're going to be grounded."

~

Child: "I don't feel like going to the party."
Adult: "You must go or Susie's feelings will be hurt."

~

Child: She crawls up the side of the play set.
Adult: "Come down here right now. You're going to fall!"

Who Is More Important?

When I was in kindergarten, my teacher Mrs. Griswold had a special "read out loud" time for the class. My class sat on the floor "Indian style" (as it was called back then) and gathered around Mrs. Griswold who read a book to the class. This weekly activity was one of my favorites.

Mrs. Griswold would read a page and then flip the book around to show the class the picture. She'd start to her left and slowly move the book across the front of her body in a semi-circle till she reached her right side. Then she'd flip the book back over, turn the page, and start reading again.

One day during reading time, a boy named Johnny kept scooting around the floor on his behind. He annoyed me. When he slid closer to me, his shoes and behind made squeaky noises so I missed some of what Mrs. Griswold said. Then he did the worst thing: He stopped moving when he got right in front of me and blocked my line of vision. I couldn't see the pictures in the book. I scowled. I was angry.

Mrs. Griswold stopped reading, put down the book, and looked at me. "Lori, if you don't like the book, you can go put your head down on the table." She pointed to the round table on the side of the room.

In front of the entire class, she was *punishing* me. I felt hurt and ashamed. I loved Mrs. Griswold's reading and hated Johnny's disruption. My disappointment was punished. My anger was wrong. My engagement and favorite activity were taken from me. Somebody else's desires and actions were made more important than mine. Why was Johnny free to scoot around and distract the class?

Perhaps something similar happened to you at one time. This particular experience reinforced that someone—Johnny—was more important than me. And that I would get punished for being me—the five year old who loved picture-book reading time—and those in authority such as Mrs. Griswold didn't care about the truth. Right or wrong, her perception was more important than mine. From this event and others like it, I learned to not show my dislike or express how I felt when I wasn't pleased.

Pleasing the Teacher

Here's another incident. In fourth grade, my teacher told me if I kept putting my long hair behind my ears, I would grow up to have unattractive ears that poked out. At the time, I could feel in my gut that wasn't true, even if she thought she was telling me the truth. So while in her class, I put a barrette in my hair, but anywhere else I did as I pleased. After all, it was only hair and I was only nine. But I learned to change my behavior to please her so she wouldn't pick on me in front of my whole class.

That same year, an adult told me if I didn't stop biting my nails, my fingers would look like black people's fingers. Now, what did that mean? The impression my little girl-self made out of the tone of his voice was that something bad would happen to me. I didn't get what black people had to do with it. I had an African American friend and her fingers looked nice. I looked at my fingers and thought, "My fingers will always look like my fingers no matter if I bite my nails or not."

Obviously, this adult who tried to scare me about biting my nails was racist, but I didn't know what racism was back then. He also didn't speak the truth. He threatened me with fear to try changing my behavior. So I started hiding my fingers in his presence because I didn't want untrue things said about my behaviors or hear my friends being insulted.

I could feel the truth within me and yet these experiences (and many others) eventually wore me down. I learned to accept what those in authority told me as truth. How I was treated created subconscious lies within me, forming a foundation from which I created my life.

Commands from my teachers and parents may have been well meaning but they didn't communicate positive intentions or tell the truth. Their directives essentially taught me the truth didn't matter and neither did I. That taught me something bad would happen if I did what I wanted. In every case, I believed the adults knew better (even if they did not).

Truthful Communication

Parents and caregivers have fears that direct them to stop children from doing what comes naturally to them. I get this; I have raised two children. A child might want to jump on the bed, walk in the stream, or play a sport, and the parent might say something like "Don't do (fill in the blank); you're going to fall/get hurt/get sick/or whatever."

Clearly, the parent is afraid the child will get hurt. But a more accurate communication would be, "I'm afraid you are going to fall so don't jump on the bed." That type of truthful communication is rare.

From innocent enough experiences like these, children learn they can't trust themselves. They learn that what they feel can't be true because the adult—Mommy, Daddy, Caregiver, Teacher—says it isn't. Or if they do what comes naturally, then they'll get hurt or be punished. Thus, why do what they want or what's natural?

Through the childhood years, these innocent directives weaken the connection between us and our inner truth. Eventually, false beliefs replace that inner truth and a pattern emerges. We learn to care more about what the other person needs/wants/believes than what we do.

My false belief? I grew up being overly responsible for the world. I came last.

Conditional Answers

In my early years in therapy and in coaching, my response to the question "How do you feel, Lori?" was "I don't know" because I didn't. Or I'd respond by saying "I think." But *how I felt* had nothing to do with *what I thought*. My typical answer was what I call a conditional directive. Here's an example dialog:

"How do you feel about that, Lori?"

"Oh, uhm, I'm not sure. I guess, well, I think maybe I feel like it was the wrong thing to do."

In the unlikely event I could answer with how I felt—with how I *truly* felt—I was still compelled to explain *why* I felt that way. When I did make a choice that honored me, I was compelled to defend my decision. Subconsciously, I believed being me or feeling what I felt was *not* okay. Never standing in the light of truth had become a long-learned pattern.

My childhood taught me that punishment followed innocent, natural actions. If my feet got wet while in the yard on a rainy day, my father would spank me because I was "bad." When I tripped down our narrow stairwell and landed at the bottom hurt and crying, instead of being cuddled and booboos kissed, my father yanked me to my feet and struck me with his belt. "I told you not to play on the steps!"

My childhood also taught me I'd receive praise for *what I did* rather than *who I was*. When my father played pinochle and gin rummy with his male friends, I'd get the job of making coffee for the men. In return, my dad was nice, and he'd give me a nickel or a dime for each cup of coffee. I learned that positive attention meant doing something for the grownups. I had to have a purpose that was defined by others.

Before I hit puberty, I also learned that if my breasts were not big enough or I wasn't pretty enough (according to somebody else's definition), I was left out of the party. I was told that by some of my sister's male friends who were five years older than me. Even in the company of girls in gym class, I was always last to be picked for a team. The message? I simply wasn't good enough being me.

When Father Left Our Family

Along with the physical punishment my father frequently doled out, he also was affectionate. He sang songs, played with us, built furniture for our cat, and took me fishing. I loved my father. So when he left our family (I was nine years old), I felt devastated, scared, and sad.

My mother was scared, too. One day when she felt overcome with despair, she cried out through the thin walls of her bedroom that had no door, "I want to kill myself! Why am I alive?" Hearing that, I froze in horror. My dad was gone; I didn't want my mom to go away, too. She might kill herself if I let her know how scared and sad I was, and I didn't want to provide the "tipping point" for her suicide.

I also believed that if she was willing to kill herself, I must not be worth living for. And if my father could leave me, I didn't have value to him either. Imagine what a huge burden I carried at nine years of age. The patterns I'd learned—not sharing how I felt, believing it was wrong to be me, others were more important than me, and my feelings weren't important—were being reinforced on a daily basis.

In addition to establishing a pattern of disassociating with my inner truth in my family, I received similar messages from other places: adult neighbors, TV shows, lessons at school and church. *It was wrong to be me.* I also learned that women couldn't hold certain jobs because of various unspoken rules in society and spoken rules in church. So just being born—born in sin—came with an inherent wrongness of being. This little girl already experiencing heartbreak needed forgiveness and redemption just for being alive. As a result, as a young adult even (while I was physically abused), I would pray at night asking for forgiveness. Lying in bed in the dark with bruises or open wounds or fear for my safety, I needed some type of redemption. After all, *something was wrong with me from the moment I was born.*

Then There's Anger

Anger has a bad rap. When we're conditioned to disassociate from our inner truth and taught that anger is bad, well, the road to heaven on earth is paved with quicksand.

Mostly, I learned the definition of anger from my parents. My father's anger erupted fast and fiercely in the form of physical punishment. My mother's anger was pushed down into a painful passive silence.

> *As a child, I believed anger was awful, traumatic, and wrong—a definition literally beaten into me.*

As children, many of us learn to define rage, violence, meanness, or abuse as anger. But it's none of these. I had reasons to be angry almost every day, but I had to disconnect from it because, in my world, how I felt didn't matter. Anger was taboo. We do what we need to be safe and survive, even if our perception of needing to survive is wrong. And I'm not talking about living in a war zone. I'm referring to everyday life in America.

We do ourselves a great disservice when we make anger an enemy, when we disown our own anger or prioritize someone else's wellbeing over our own. We can't create a fulfilling life when we put anger on a "do not touch" shelf. Nor can we thrive without the healthy emotional energy of anger.

Anger's Bad Rap and Our Responses

Spiritual teachers often talk about anger being a low vibrational energy that prevents spiritual growth. Here, a distinction needs to be made between the *healthy* emotional energy of anger and an unconscious, negative reaction that manifests as blame, negative thinking, and the appearance of a reactive, violent energy. Emotional integrity is required for spiritual growth so judging our anger as wrong will limit us on the spiritual path.

Here's what is true: The inner truth of anger felt as a sensation will never tell you that someone else is responsible for your life. If you feel angry in that way, there's a disconnect with what's going on *inside* of you compared with *outside* of you long before the latest episode of displeasure occurred.

For me—and by presenting the healthy approach to being a bitch—I point out the difference between the healthy emotional energy of anger and reacting to anger. The inner truth of anger needs to be noticed and honored, and our response is based on what we need in the moment.

We simply need to know how the inner sensation of anger feels, what that experience is like, and what wisdom it's trying to impart.

> *We can't honor anger if we don't know what it is when it's created inside of us.*

Once we establish a habit of ignoring how we feel, our choices usually benefit somebody else better than they do us. Or perhaps no one at all. Yet overriding what we feel and therefore what we need invalidates us. That's when an outward expression of anger replaces our inner truth.

Ignoring our anger is an injustice, a violation, to the self. I will boldly say this: Overriding our anger is self-abuse. And ironically, when we override our truth, we tend to get mad at others or become the victim of someone's projected anger.

What is happening? When we dishonor ourselves and how we feel, we behave as unconscious role models showing people how we want to be treated—that is, with dishonor. We treat ourselves how we want others to treat us.

> *When we're disconnected from our inner truth, unsure how we feel, and unaware of our needs or wants, our intentions can be wishy washy. We struggle to make decisions in our lives.*

An Example of the Struggle

I lived in a historic home for twenty-two years. During this time, I hired roofers, carpenters, painters, and other contractors for remodeling, maintenance, and troubleshooting.

For many of those years and with several of the contractors, I was afraid to speak my truth. When the carpenter did sloppy work or the painter missed a part of the wood trim, I secretly freaked out inside. In the early years, I kept my mouth shut because I was afraid to tell the contractor about my dissatisfaction. Subconsciously, I believed I was responsible for his emotional wellbeing and if I disappointed someone, my safety could be in jeopardy. I also believed (subconsciously) what I felt or wanted was less important than what the other person wanted, that those contractors wanted to just go home after a day of work.

So I bit my tongue rather than simply say to the painter, "Hey, you missed a spot." Instead, I'd say something like, "Sorry to bother you, but if you have a moment, I'd like to show you something. It's not that important, but if you have some time and agree, perhaps you could add a little more paint to that area of the wood trim. I know not many people will see it, and I know I'm picky and everything. Or you could also leave behind some paint so I could do it myself later. Thanks so much."

No matter the situation, I could feel my body close down and tighten. I'd jump into my head and rationalize away why what I wanted (and paid for) wasn't that important.

A Boundaries Example

During the years I lived in the Pennsylvania farmhouse, I had twelve neighbors whose land butted up to mine. When new people moved into the neighborhood, they started cutting trees down along the property line. Believing they weren't clear about the legal boundaries, I had a survey drawn and flags stuck in the earth. They went ahead anyway and put up a structure with part of it built on my property. An immense sensation in my body was yelling, "Tell them to stop." I felt angry because my boundaries were being violated—*and* I felt afraid to tell them about it.

Over and over, my property boundaries were violated. Over and over, I stressed about telling them. Again, my subconscious beliefs played out:

"The other person's wellbeing is more important than mine."

"If I disappoint these people, my safety will be in jeopardy."

When I told my neighbors their workers had cut my dog's underground electric fence after they planted a bush on my property, they said I shouldn't have installed the wire so close to the edge of my property. My property! I was shown again that if I didn't honor myself, the world wouldn't either.

My neighbors and I eventually solved our boundary issues, but we could only do so when I got to that point of feeling my inner truth and honoring it. My inner conflict was mirrored by the conflict I had with my neighbors.

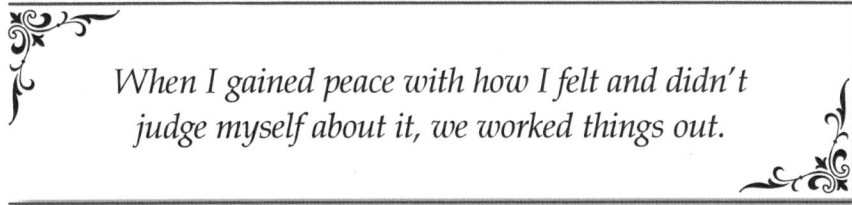

When I gained peace with how I felt and didn't judge myself about it, we worked things out.

Loving, Safe Presence

A few years ago, I dated a wonderful man named David. Even though I'd transformed many of my false subconscious beliefs, some still lingered, and his loving, safe presence helped me work through more of them.

Here's an example. The first night I invited him to spend the night, he waited for me to finish my bedtime routine. I still had on my evening dress, and I needed to wash my face and brush my teeth. I could feel anxiety as I stepped into the bathroom and thought, "How selfish of me to invite him over and leave him alone." So I stepped out the bathroom, went over to him, and said, "I'm sorry, but I want to wash my face and brush my teeth. Or I could just forget about it for the night if that's better for you."

Yes, I said that. The main man in my life had immediately taken over as the authority figure in my subconscious. But he simply said, "Do what you need to do, Lori. What makes you think it's not okay to take care of yourself?"

What a question! I didn't answer it fully that night, but eventually I told him what made me think it wasn't okay to take care of myself. In circumstances far less selfish, I had been beaten, strangled, and yelled at. I had to keep myself safe and keep things peaceful. Though I wasn't forced to live that way any longer, my subconscious mind and habits kept that behavior alive.

Bonafide Bitches

In situations when we're not threatened but react as though we are, we need to be bonafide bitches for ourselves. That's when we must be heroic, honorable, and powerful using the weapon of empowerment—self-love. And self-love requires gentleness and compassion.

After living with Craig and being abused weekly for several years, I became well trained to conform with his demands and mental illness. When I went to work or college or the grocery store, he timed me to the minute. If I didn't arrive home when he thought I should, he came looking for me. The consequences of being late resulted in bruises on my body and violent vocalized accusations.

ANGER 101

After I left this relationship, it took me more than two years to stop at an ATM and not be filled with anxiety about being late—a symptom of PTSD that I suffered with for years. Even today, I occasionally hear an inner whisper that says "hurry up" when I get ready to go out or come home.

When conditions like these have been figuratively or literally beaten into us, we must be extra gentle and loving with ourselves. Habits and beliefs have a biological component. Our brains form neural networks based on our training, conditioning, and experiences. Whatever we are taught, true or untrue, takes up neural real estate, and replacing that biological creation takes time, practice, and awareness. It's because of our human brain that we can override our inner truth in the first place. It's also because of our brain that we can reprogram new, positive life habits that honor our inner truth.

Our subconscious may be invisible to the naked eye, but it's always in the driver seat. That's why it's important to be aware of habits and patterns in our lives. An example is my stressful, conditioned reaction about getting home late even when I didn't live with Craig.

When we are aware of what isn't working for us, we can start to change our lives. We can't change our subconscious subconsciously; we can only change our subconscious *consciously*. That is, with conscious practice, we can learn Embodied Awareness and be connected to our inner truth as a way of life. With practice, we can also reprogram our brain with more heroic, honorable, and powerful ways to live.

Yes, this reprogramming takes time. The biology of being human is complex. Loving patience helps us transform the energy of lies into living truth.

When the lies you are living are triggered, they may trip you up, but the power of the truth forms a stronger army.

*When you commit to your inner truth,
its power will move you forward.*

TIME FOR YOUR TRUTH

To start, practice at least one minute of grounding. (See Introduction for Grounding Exercise instructions.) Then ask the following questions one at a time. Be curious and be gentle. After asking each question, close your eyes and *feel* into each answer.

Write down your answers and insights, taking special note of those that yield the strongest sensations in your body. I recommend answering them by speaking into a voice recorder on your smartphone or other device. You would review them while practicing Embodied Awareness. (See Introduction for instructions on Embodied Awareness.)

1) Do you ever use the word "feel" to describe your thoughts, opinions, or ideas? Do you ever use the word "think" to describe how you feel?
2) Have you ever been taught or told that what you feel is incorrect or wrong? Describe in detail this experience.
3) Are there times when you don't allow yourself to take care of yourself when you need to? Describe this situation and be curious about your choice.
4) Are you aware of any false subconscious beliefs that formed when you were a child that direct your behavior these days? What are they and how do they affect your life?
5) Have you noticed any negative repeating patterns in your life? If so, describe them. If not, notice any repeating struggles that you haven't been able to rid yourself of.

SUGGESTED PRACTICE

Again, practice at least one minute of grounding and then take these actions:

- If you answered yes in the first question above, be intentional using the word "feel" when you're communicating about what you feel concerning your body. Be intentional using the word "think" when you're communicating about your thoughts, ideas, and opinions.
- Choose an area of your life that is asking you to be heroic, honorable, and powerful. Practice Embodied Awareness and the Acknowledgment Cycle (see instructions in Introduction). Take inspired action for that area. It can be as simple as taking fifteen minutes to soak in a bath when others are asking for your time and attention, or telling your friends/neighbors how you feel about their behavior. You'll know right away what needs your attention, so be gentle with yourself and don't talk yourself out of your truth. After completing your inspired action, write down or record how you feel.
- Celebrate being heroic, honorable, and powerful for yourself.

Conscious Choice and Courage

The Whisper of Something More

Being born human is a multi-faceted and complex topic. Obviously I'm not alone in my curiosity because there are tens of thousands of books about the psychology, physiology, and spirituality of the human infant, child, and adult. Perhaps millions.

Since the age of seven, I've read thousands of books exploring the condition of the human personality, body, and soul. I wanted to know what made us tick. Underlying my curiosity about humanity was a compelling desire to heed Socrates' directive to Know Thyself and specifically learn what made me tick.

Every time I got hit over the head with trauma, I would reel once again in shock and emotional pain. Why did this happen? Thankfully, the books I read have helped create an intellectual understanding of the intricacies of being human and relationship. The lessons assisted me in making different choices with greater awareness so that abuse and violence happened less—and ceased to be present. And yet, the underlying belief and habits remained.

Books written about relationships were meant to help people heal and grow their bond. But for me, the "other" in the relationship wasn't interested in transforming it. Many times I wanted the "other" to change because I incorrectly assumed that, after that change, all would be well. When I did approach my partner, I received feedback that he was right and I was wrong. There was no room in his consciousness to consider healing, growth, or change.

> *As long as I focused on him, though, I closed myself off to true transformation.*

Since partnership work wasn't viable in any of my early relationships, then these relationships weren't sustainable. Eventually, I focused on myself. I read books about abusers, narcissists, addicts, and people like me who entered into relationships with people like them. In that case, I learned that I didn't have a sense of self. Who was I, after all? What was important *to* me *for* me?

Meditation Practice

In 1998, I met Dr. Deepak Chopra at the Chopra Center for Wellbeing. I learned Primordial Sound Meditation from his partner, the late Dr. Simon. I stayed at the Center for four days. Before I returned home, I purchased a few books from the Chopra bookstore to help me along my journey. When I got home, I immediately started a meditation practice. Each day for thirty minutes, I sat in silence and practiced the mantra Dr. Simon had given me.

Following a beautiful prayer and meditation ritual has helped create miracles in my life.

Meditation helped me get through the court dates, the discussions, the divorce, and the co-parenting challenges with my children's father for the next sixteen years. My practice helped me grow my awareness and expand my consciousness.

Meditation and my growing awareness helped me depersonalize the actions of others and empower myself—*yet I still drew to me men who would not honor me.* Subconscious beliefs and cellular memory held within my body still drew trauma and heartache to me. That told me I still wasn't connected to my inner truth of wisdom or my anger.

Coach Chris

It was only through coaching and somatic therapy that I opened to the truth within me and discovered what I was looking for. Through coaching, I learned that an inner truth was alive and well within me. Specifically, my coach Chris Laiguno helped me learn about me—to get *out of* my intellect and *into* my body. He taught me how to connect to my body's *wisdom* so I could then connect to my soul self.

Session after session and homework after homework, I worked on Embodied Awareness. Chris's patience and support anchored me into a practice of getting grounded in my body. As I connected to the inner truth and trauma within, I shared with him intimate, emotional experiences and received continuous support.

Sharing with a man in this way seemed scary to me, and I put up great resistance at first. Chris showed me a man can be present, be safe, and be loving to a woman in need. He never pushed me to go where I wasn't ready. I intentionally brought my embodied traumas to him so I could show my scared self that trusting a trustworthy man was safe—that I could trust Chris.

I knew that learning to trust was required for my healing. Now that I'm a coach, I know how wonderfully present and supportive coaches are because I am, too. Chris's unconditional, safe support allowed me to be with what was within me, acknowledge it, and honor it—no matter how scared I felt.

> *Though I continued to read books, I learned most about myself by going right to the source: the wisdom stored and communicated within my body.*

Connect to Inner Wisdom and Soul

During my time with Chris, I learned the difference between *intellectual* awareness/consciousness and the *embodied* version. If awareness isn't embodied, the head still plays the main role and will either override, ignore, or judge the truth. This transformed my life.

My innate desire to know myself was only achieved through practicing Embodied Awareness. I could experience myself in each moment by witnessing what was going on in my body in situations of reacting with fear and conditioned habits. I was able to make conscious choices rather than habitual ones.

Connecting to my inner truth and the stored trauma within resulted in having a more loving relationship with myself. As I created this loving connection, my relationships with others also became more mutually fulfilling and loving. The more I honored my truth, the more others honored me.

A book such as this one can point you to your inner truth, explain it intellectually, suggest practices to get in touch with it, and inspire or intrigue you to explore expanded awareness. But ultimately the only way to know yourself is by experiencing the fullness of who you are, willingly and with love.

Similarly, a book *cannot* outline what untruths your life is conforming to or how specifically those untruths were created. But it might help you become more aware that false beliefs exist in your subconscious and explain how the subconscious is always in the driver's seat.

So let me state the obvious: This book is not the Holy Grail. However, somewhere within it, I hope you find the inspiration and support you need to experience the most powerful truth that resides in the most sacred place—right inside of you. And the only way to connect to your inner truth is through Embodied Awareness.

> *When a person practices Embodied Awareness, life is filled with more grace and ease, and less struggle.*

Coach Invites and Ignites Answers

A good coach helps you grow your awareness and deepen your learning about *yourself*. A good coach takes all that "stuff" you want to talk about, complain about, learn about, and brings you home to *you*.

A coach doesn't suggest solutions to a client's issues but instead offers powerful questions and a presence that invites and ignites the answers already within you. Coaches focus on the power and wholeness of their clients so they can Know Thyself in a way that would make the ancient Greeks proud.

One book that is an exception in my quest to Know Thyself is this one. As I travel along this writing journey, so many untruths about me are being uncovered. These untruths have caused me great fear and anxiety. Sharing stories of trauma and transformation has triggered multiple sensations of emotional energies—so many that I've had to practice being grounded, leaning into what I feel and responding authentically.

When I feel stuck writing, at first I want to get mad, but then I compassionately connect with what's going on in my body. I get up and move. I dance, play, and even cry. As I wrote this manuscript, unacknowledged trauma energy within me came up, and I even coached with Chris again.

As I write these words, I practice all the processes I suggest because I know they work.

Untruths Hang On

Writing *Anger 101* has been illuminating. My false subconscious beliefs are scurrying like a bunch of cockroaches suddenly exposed to the light of day and trying to hide. But once exposed, the next step is pest control. The untruths try hanging on tight, but they can only start to lose their grip on my reality. "I have to be perfect." "I can't disappoint anyone." "I can't fail." "I don't want people to think bad of me." "Everything is such effort, and I don't want to do any of it."

Those untruths are headed to their place in my history and booted off the journey to my future. Similarly, I'm rediscovering all the true qualities about my life I adore: being vulnerable, compassionate, committed to myself, wanting to serve others, and more.

Written Reflections

While writing, I dance between personal and impersonal consciousness. I go from being overwhelmed to being amazed; from the darkest valley to the highest peak. It's a constant to and fro from fear to light-heartedness.

Sometimes, I write about being in quicksand while feeling like I *am* in the quicksand. Other times, it's more like "hey, I'm writing about quicksand and while I feel like I'm writing while I'm in quicksand, I know I'm not in quicksand."

I recommend all people write books about themselves or at least journal regularly because written reflection is powerful. So is committing to a goal. When we make a commitment to anything, and especially to ourselves, obstacles in the way of our goal show up. *As you commit to your inner truth, you expose the lies you're living.*

What do you do? Make a commitment to live authentically and, without a doubt, all the falsehoods, fears, doubts, and other limitations will show up. The lies are hanging on for dear life so when you commit to banishing them, they show up in battle gear.

But without your belief in them, they cannot live. Still, you need the falsehoods to become apparent; otherwise, you won't know they're still present. You need to see the cockroaches in the light because they aren't visible in the dark. You need to reveal what's hiding in the darkness—what's living in your subconscious—to choose the light, to choose truth, and to choose consciously.

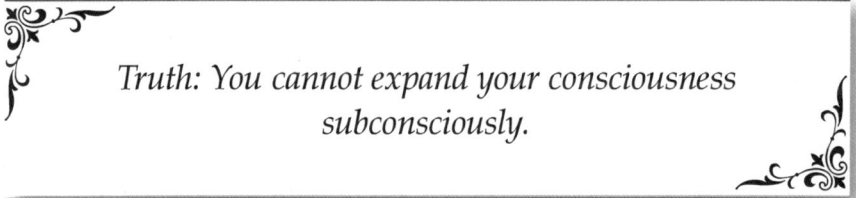

Truth: You cannot expand your consciousness subconsciously.

Exposing a Living Lie

Deepening your learning about what makes you tick subconsciously will lead you to discover where you disassociate with your inner truth. Sometimes when a living lie gets exposed, becoming *aware* of that lie is enough to start unraveling it. And sometimes when we're early in our journey of self-awareness, we need to understand the how, what, why, and when—mostly because our mind wants to understand the unexpressed emotional energy; it's an intellectual pursuit.

But through understanding comes compassion. And through compassion, we are more willing to go into our bodies and connect to that old energy within. That old energy is attached to the past experiences of our lives. And by acknowledging that old energy, we can transform it as we let go of the past.

Change is a natural consequence of reconnecting to your inner truth. That's what you want: change. *Reconnecting to your inner truth will transform your life.* Transforming your life transforms relationships: the relationship you have with yourself and your relationship with everyone and everything else, too.

Expanding into more authenticity comes at the loss of outgrown-outworn-outdated parts, roles, and habits you have lived, so you will experience loss. It may feel like you take a few steps forward and then a few steps back. What is really happening? The cycle of expansion and contraction. Loss and rebirth.

> *Consciously choosing truth when you have lived with subconscious lies for most of your life is consciously choosing a death of sorts.*

Expand Our Comfort Zone

When we reconnect to our inner truth, we also choose to expand our comfort zone. The two go hand in hand. And this unknown horizon is scary for we've not been there before. Living a lie may be uncomfortable but at least we know what to expect.

Being in our comfort zone leads to the same direction with the same roads with a perceived sense of safety. But when we're on the edge of our comfort zone, we need the energy of courage to move us through our fear of going beyond what we know. On that edge, we can learn so much about ourselves—*as long as we don't judge our experience and shrink back.*

Choosing consciously to expand our comfort zone automatically expands our consciousness and fulfillment. As we let go of those disharmonious old ways, we may find that our lives feel empty, that we are alone, that something is missing. We may experience a dark night of the soul, but in this case, it is darkest before the dawn. This feeling of loneliness and even temporary despair will pass—as long as you remain in Embodied Awareness.

To speak our inner truth to the outside world can be scary when we're not used to doing that. This practice of honoring inner truths will likely need to be a discipline until authentically responding to the moment becomes natural. When I start to feel discomfort, I occasionally jump into my head, disassociate with what I'm feeling, switch my attention to something that generates less discomfort, get caught up in a story, or try to figure something out. Nowadays, I don't need as much courage to live authentically as I did; I just need reminders.

Along with needing reminders to be present with my inner truth, I also remind myself to trust myself, to be gentle and loving with myself.

Learning about the conditions of the human organism has led me to have a growing compassion for us humans. My heart has opened wider while my rational brain has chilled out. We humans are living our lives as we have been designed. We are doing the best we can at the level of our consciousness. The awesome thing is, if something isn't working for us, with awareness, we can change and create a whole new way of living that *does* work for us. That's where teachers, books, coaches, and mentors can help. Those wise guideposts along the journey can support us as we reconnect to the wisdom that has been ours all along.

Why We Disassociate

There is a simple reason why we have become disconnected from our inner truth. It's this: After birth, we start to experience the rules of life others have created long before we were conceived. We are taught that disassociating from our inner truth is the way to be. We learn that we can't trust ourselves. We're convinced how we feel is wrong and that someone (everyone) is more important than us. In effect, we override what we feel.

Our upbringing teaches us the original lies as well as any truths to live by. We continue with learned beliefs until we figure out there's something more. That "something more" is the whisper of our inner truth—always alive, always calling our name, always ready to be liberated when we're ready for spiritual growth.

Though our inner truth is as organic as breathing, unlike our need for oxygen it can be dismissed. That's why our autonomic nervous system handles breathing and all the other life-and-death functions for us. We are born full of our divine truth and then conditioned with what we learn so our divine truth is hidden from view.

No one can ever take our truth from us, and no matter how much we ignore it, it cannot die or be destroyed. However, it can be habitually overridden until it seems it doesn't exist anymore.

Fortunately, we have the rest of our lives as our human selves to return home to our truth.

Trust Yourself

Just about everyone has something to say in what we should believe and how we should live. I hesitate to add one more opinion to the all too many that already litter our consciousness, but I share my experience anyway. My message is this: *Ultimately trust yourself.* Your golden inner truth is always there, whenever you want to connect with it, listen to it, honor it, love it. More loyal and loving than your BFF, it's your secret, and only you can hear it whisper. Your inner truth needs no explanation, algebraic formula, or religion to define it in its standalone fullness.

If what I share here resonates with you, that's great. Explore that resonance in the sacredness of your own being. You will benefit by that experience.

If what I share here does *not* resonate with you, that's great too. Explore that dissonance in the sacredness of your own being. You will greatly benefit by that experience.

Please trust yourself on that. I never want to override what is true for you.

TIME FOR YOUR TRUTH

To start, practice at least one minute of grounding. (See Introduction for Grounding Exercise instructions.) Then ask the following questions one at a time. Be curious and be gentle. After asking each question, close your eyes and *feel* into each answer.

Write down your answers and insights, taking special note of those that yield the strongest sensations in your body. I recommend answering them by speaking into a voice recorder on your smartphone or other device. You would review them while practicing Embodied Awareness. (See Introduction for instructions on Embodied Awareness.)

1) Do you have a relationship with someone and you wish the other person would change in some way? Practice the Acknowledgment Cycle (See Introduction for Acknowledgment Cycle instructions) and answer these questions: What wants to

happen? Who is this experience asking you to be? What is this experience asking you to do?

2) Do you have a holistic practice that supports you in challenging times? If not, what supportive practice might you create for yourself? Consider movement, meditation, prayer, etc.

3) What quality would you like to receive from others? How might you give this *to* yourself *from* yourself?

4) What "whisper of something more" for your life do you hear? When do you hear it? What is that "whisper of something more" asking you to be, to do?

5) What one situation have you been thinking about that you have to figure out these days? Take five minutes to Practice Embodied Awareness and the Acknowledgment Cycle to help you see what your inner truth already knows about this situation.

SUGGESTED PRACTICE

Again, practice at least one minute of grounding and then take these actions:

- Take time to journal about an experience that causes you discomfort. Practice Embodied Awareness when writing. Take a break if you need to. Ground yourself and continue writing. Be gentle and compassionate with yourself. When you are finished, what did you learn that you didn't know before you started writing?
- Choose a time in your daily experience when being grounded with Embodied Awareness and the Acknowledgment Cycle are needed. Choose an anchor to have with you: a symbol, an item, some type of reminder to get grounded, to honor yourself, and be with your inner wisdom.
- Celebrate your commitment to yourself.

Honoring the Truth

Accepting the Self

Being in touch with how we feel and letting this truth guide us would seem to be authentic, organic, and completely natural. For some, it is. For too many others (including me for over half of my life), we've learned to ignore, suppress, and deny how we feel—especially if we are feeling anger. Having learned the habit of dissociating with our feelings, we are pros at not listening to our inner truth no matter how urgent the need might be.

It's easy to fall back into old habits that disregard our inner truth. These usually lifelong habits make us ignore our inner truth that exists in the moment. When we ignore our inner truth, it's impossible to be connected with it. And without connection, there's no honoring of ourselves.

Ignoring, denying, and judging how we feel imprisons the repressed emotion in our shadow self.

What's in the shadows controls our lives.

The goal is to bring our truth, our beliefs, our fears into the light. In the light, all layers of our truth can be seen, acknowledged, and honored.

ANGER 101

When is the perfect time for honoring the truth? All the time in each moment every day. With each breath. Right now.

Similarly, the perfect time for accepting yourself is now. When you acknowledge and accept your truth—and therefore yourself—you're in your most powerful state of being, a state in which life flows with grace and ease.

Our Inner Most GPS

The feeling of anger may be the feeling we distance ourselves from the most. And yet, the healthy emotional energy of anger always shows us when and how we need ourselves the most.

Anger is like the voice of our innermost GPS that says, "Follow the route" or "Make a U-turn" when we make a wrong turn or believe our way isn't as important as another way. The healthy emotional energy of anger always guides us in the direction of our North Star like a spirit guide and trusted advisor.

We'd be smart to have a serious intimate relationship with our anger.

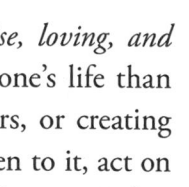

I can't say this enough: *Anger as our inner voice is wise, loving, and honorable.* There's no better ally along the journey of one's life than that. Anger is not about blaming others, hurting others, or creating any type of violence. When we're in touch with it—listen to it, act on it—we're better able to create a life of integrity and fulfillment. We live in integrity when what we speak, do, and think are all on the same page—when we are one with our truth.

Conversely, when we judge our anger, we create duality within, separating ourselves from our truth. We create a house divided. And the more we separate ourselves from our truth, life will continue to create experiences that try to crack us open to allow the treasure within to come out and be honored.

Know this: We cannot be our fully empowered selves when we're out of alignment with our truth, because in that dissonance, we stack the odds against us. Thus, accepting our inner truth is accepting ourselves. And that acceptance is a requirement for inner power.

When we're in integrity, we become a healthy conduit that can fully express our divine purpose. But if we ignore, deny, or judge our inner truth, we're not fully present or able to grow into higher dimensions of spiritual truth. Closing ourselves off from any part of our being limits us from spiritual growth and maturity. Cutting ourselves off from our inner truth of anger fills the road to spiritual enlightenment with dead ends, frustration, and exhaustion.

Ignoring our truth is not an easy road to travel, but it's an oft-traveled path.

Connecting with our anger would do a world of good. Literally. The world would know more peace if we as individuals experienced more inner peace. If we ignore, deny, or judge our anger, what happens? We project our anger on to others and become angry with them. Or ourselves. As my friend and coach Chris Liaguno says, "Let us be aware of our inner conflict before we project war unto others."

Break Free into a Greater Reality

The potential to honor your anger and accept the self lies in each moment. Awareness that something more is available to you is key to the unfolding of limitations. When you're no longer willing to live an unfulfilling life, it's time to break free into a greater reality. And that reality includes the healthy approach to being a bitch. It's about the healthy emotional energy of anger—about accepting, acknowledging, and honoring your inner truth.

For me, the cyclical process of acknowledging, accepting, and honoring my inner truth is an everyday practice. It's as natural as breathing, and that still happily surprises me because after almost thirty years at ignoring my inner truth, when it happens naturally, I am grateful.

Other times, heeding the wisdom of my inner truth is an intentional process. And sometimes it's a consequence of feeling discomfort with what's going on in my life, the consequences of unconscious choices. It's at these times I can feel that familiar sensation of anger within, but the habit of ignoring it prevailed in that experience.

Many of us get the opportunity to honor our anger and accept the self only when life cracks us open—and only if we can see what's happening with new eyes of awareness. These life experiences happen by divine design; if we aren't honoring ourselves, life creates a breaking point, usually a trauma that's like a rapid avalanche trying to get our attention. We run like hell to avoid being buried or trapped, but just running away won't change a thing.

> *The gift of trauma means being shocked into awareness that we have a more powerful and authentic way to live—one that requires our inner truth.*

My Gifts of Trauma

For the first half of my life, repeated traumas became the catalyst that broke me open to my inner truth. Deeper and deeper. Reminder after reminder. Pain and suffering, again and again. Today, my life lessons come more gently. Every now and again, though, the bigger experiences in life show me how I can love myself more. Trauma isn't always a requirement to be the catalyst for spiritual and emotional growth. We can consciously choose expanded consciousness as a life practice—a practice that's gentle.

I experienced my biggest breaking point when I was thirty-five years old while being the best mother and wife I could be and living the best life I'd ever lived. Each week, I wrote in my gratitude journal with humble declarations about my blessed life. I was so in love with my life. And then it happened.

Just a few years after I married and became a mother of two children, I found myself rejected and alone—a participant in a traumatic divorce I did not want. One day, I'd be writing in my gratitude journal and the next reeling from feelings of abandonment, rejection, and judgment.

Yet again I was shown, told, and believed that my effort wasn't enough; *who I was* was somehow wrong and unfulfilling for my husband. The shocking dissolution of my marriage became a wakeup call, my biggest breaking point. I simply couldn't allow my children to inherit the heartbreaking patterns of my life. I was fed up with ending last in a game I never wanted to play, and I certainly didn't want the same for my children.

Becoming a Bitch Through Karate

During this time, my therapist suggested I try karate to get in touch with fear and build my confidence. I heeded her suggestion and joined a Tang Soo Do karate studio ten minutes from my house. That's when my healthy approach to becoming a bitch began in earnest.

The first practice I was taught in karate was bowing to the teachers and black belts, always answering them with a "No, Sir!" or a "Yes, Sir!" Yet everyone in the class appeared younger than me, and everyone was a stranger. This forced honor and respect seemed wrong. Besides, I had been forced to give honor, respect, and loyalty to others most of my life,

ANGER 101

and it had never worked in my favor. The start of training seemed as if I was being made less than someone else—again.

But before the first week finished, not only was I bowing down to black belts they were bowing down to me. The karate teachers treated me with honor and set the stage for all students and teachers to honor one another. My teachers expected everyone in the *dojang* (formal training hall) to be our best selves no matter what. I met their expectations and exceeded my own.

My first teaching by the late Master DiPietro was "If you are confronted with conflict, walk away if possible. You don't need karate for that. But if walking away is not an option, I will teach you to protect yourself and disarm the person who assaults you."

Before the end of the free month tryout, I got in touch with an inner power that told me no one had the right to hurt me, take from me, or dishonor me. The punching and kicking of the target also unleashed a passion and anger that had been silent for too long. We were required to kiap, which is the exhaled power of chi (energy) used with intention to focus our inner power. A kiap naturally touches into the core center of chi and puts the martial artist into the most powerful state of being.

At first I felt embarrassed to kiap because of its loud vocalization. But embarrassment had no chance for survival. The kiap reached down deep into my will center and third chakra. The energy rose through my body and came out through my throat and fifth chakra. A sense of being a more powerful me quickly replaced any embarrassment. I was desperate to be a more powerful me.

The sleeping lioness was finally wakened.
I was done being a silent victim.

How Karate Supported Me

Karate naturally supported me in a journey to undo the training that started at three-and-a-half years old. It taught me that *I mattered*. I felt treated with honor, respect, and equality. I was less than no one—and I didn't even have to earn it!

From this training, I learned to create an energetic and physical boundary around my personal space, to protect myself in the moment. Practicing karate included sparring and all the techniques we learned: kicking, punching, blocks, falls, and throws. When I'd spar and land punches or kicks on my opponent, I felt awful. After all, my life had been focused on taking care of everyone else and making sure I didn't impose discomfort on others. In those moments of landing punches and kicks, I'd stop sparring. I'd let my arms drop low leaving my solar plexus, chest, and head unprotected, and then I'd apologize to my opponent. "I'm sorry. Are you okay?"

Through the mouth piece that protected the teeth, the cushioned helmet that protected the head and face, and the gloves held up in front of the chin protecting the throat, the muffled response was always "Yeah." Affirming my opponent's okayness was usually followed by an easy landing of a punch or kick to my vulnerable, unprotected body.

My concern for my opponents' wellbeing over my own resulted in soreness and bruising from their punches and kicks.

My karate brothers and sisters focused on themselves as they should have, while my focus should have been on my own safety and technique. When I fell into the habit of devaluing my safety (and therefore myself) and made the other person more important, I suffered in sparring—just like I suffered in my relationships with men.

Divorce and Resistance

The divorce proceedings started when my children were only two and four years old. It seemed they were forced to visit and stay overnight with their father long before they were ready. For sure, it was long before *I* was ready, despite my first lawyer saying, "They'll get used to it."

Their resistance wasn't because they didn't love their father but because of so much change. They were young and not ready to be separated from me, a stay-at-home mommy who cared for them full time. Also, they adored their grandfather who lived with us at the time. And they wanted to be with their pets in the comfort of the only family home they'd known. I'm sure they could feel my sense of loss, distress, and resistance, too.

On Christmas Eve 1999, my five-year-old daughter was sick in bed all day with a high fever. She had no appetite or energy. Would I have to spend Christmas in the emergency room with her? That concerned me, but I was more stressed out about having to tell her father she was sick and couldn't spend Christmas Day with him. I was afraid he'd be upset with me and blame me. But I had to tell him. I had to do what was best for our daughter, no matter how scared I felt contacting him.

Standing in the kitchen of my Pennsylvania farmhouse, I held the phone in my hands as I gazed through the sliding glass doors that looked out over the backfield. My gut and chest tightened with anxiety. I searched for a sign of life in the back field—something to inspire or distract me, to ease the stress and give me courage to call my children's father on this cold winter's day.

There was nothing but gray sky and freezing temperatures. So I did the only thing I could do. I dialed his number, held my breath, and hoped his answering machine would answer instead of him.

"Hello." He picked up.

After a tense but polite greeting, I continued in one shallow breath, "Carolynne has a fever of one-hundred-and-three. She's been in bed all day and is sleeping right now. She can't travel tomorrow. I might have to take her to the hospital."

All of me was in high alert. My sensitive hearing heard a raised voice in response to the news. I felt as if he were yelling at me. Of course, he was disappointed. In my insecurity, I was taking his words as accusing me of a made-up scheme. It seemed he was insinuating I was lying and being unfair to him. Or was I making up this guilt myself?

Whatever was going on, I knew I needed him to express a calm understanding, and I wasn't getting that. After all, I was worried about our daughter while going through this divorce and feelings of loss. It triggered every trauma in my whole life.

Then for the first time in my relationship with my husband and only a month after starting karate, I recognized a sensation of emotional energy inside of me. It *was* anger. Without thinking, I knew that *I mattered*, and that I deserved to be honored no matter what.

"This is about Carolynne," I stated firmly. "She's *not* well. I might have to take her to see a doctor on Christmas Day."

What seemed like relentless accusations continued. He'd say, "This is not fair to me! We agreed with our lawyers that I would have the children on Christmas. You can't make unilateral decisions!"

The energy that started in my solar plexus rose through my chest and throat, and it kept going until it was transformed into words, focused words from an empowered me. The silent victim was gone. Now embodied in my being was Master DiPietro's teaching: "If you are confronted with conflict, walk away if possible. You don't need karate for that. But if walking away is not an option, we will teach you to protect yourself and disarm the person who assaults you."

I said, "This is about Carolynne. Please stop speaking to me like that or I'm hanging up." The words hung in the air in front of me. For a second, I shook with fear and then courage.

He continued. I hung up.

Then I watched myself put the phone down slowly as if it were somebody else's hand—someone else's life. I didn't recognize myself. I turned around and looked out again to the gray cloudy sky, the brown of the grass, and the leafless trees. My hand went instinctively to my stomach. Noticing I was holding my breath, I exhaled.

Nothing outside had changed, but inside of me, something that had been dormant for too long was emerging.

I was changing, and a new sensation was very much alive in me. My inner truth created in that moment was a healthy sensation of emotional energy: anger. I felt the anger in my body, and I honored it. I was heroic, honorable, and powerful on my own behalf. For once, I didn't override how I really felt. I did this for myself. And for my daughter.

Then I leaned against the cold windows of the sliding doors and cried.

The Path of Self-Love

How we feel is always about our experience, our perception, and our potential. And yes, our choices. My children's father didn't create the anger in me; my body did based on my experience of life in that moment.

All my feelings are mine, created within me. My children's father unknowingly gave me an opportunity to wake up from the silent denial of my inner truth. Though the divorce was one of the most difficult times of my life, I am grateful how the consequences of my marriage failing forced me to consciously love myself. Starting down that path of self-love propelled me into becoming the woman I am now.

Today when I recall that time, I feel grateful. I know my children's father and I had a soul agreement, and we kept our promises to each other. My relationship with him helped thrust me into an ever-expanding consciousness. And the key to my expansion was the depth of my human emotion.

We have a right to how we feel and to honor what that feeling tells us. Our bodies have a wisdom that can't be silenced, but it can be denied. No matter how long we ignore, judge, or suppress our inner truth, it is always there. Subconsciously, we will continue to create life experiences that trigger our suppressed inner truth so that one day, when we come to that breaking point (or earlier), we can realize we *deserve* our very own love.

We can allow ourselves to heed the wisdom of our body and souls.

Connected to the Infinite Truth

Our wise bodies never lie to us. But so often we don't understand our own bodily wisdom. We don't even realize that it's trying to speak to us. Our culture mostly teaches us that our bodies are machines to feed and treat. We are not taught that our bodies can be a huge source of wisdom. Instead, we are shown how to ignore our body's wisdom by repressing its messages. Have a tummy ache? Take this drug. Got a headache, can't sleep? Pop this pill. Feel anxiety? Take this pill or pour an alcoholic drink. We medicate the language of the body.

When we ignore our body's wisdom enough times, we get to a point of experiencing regret, rage, disappointment, blame, depression, physical pain, stress, migraines, and more. All of those help us align with our inner truth—if we only know that's an option.

People talk about how following their hearts leads to disappointment. "I should have known better than to follow my heart," they say. The truth is, when we follow our hearts, we connect with a profound wisdom. So many people think their fears and attachments are love, and that false love comes from the heart. That mistaken egotistic identity has let them down. Yet the heart knows no fear and cannot be attached to any person, place, or thing. The truth of the heart is unconditional love for self and others.

Our higher self loves us no matter what. It allows us to do what we want even if it causes us pain and suffering. That's why we can do stupid things that go against us. Yet following the heart's desire is always honorable, because by connecting to the truth of the heart, it shows us the honorable way. One form of that is through the healthy emotional energy of anger.

Smelling a Skunk

Imagine smelling a skunk. Do you really need to think it over if you like the smell of skunk or not? No. But suppose you were raised to believe to not trust yourself. At the same time, you were told by those closest to you in authority positions that skunk spray smelled good. Then you were punished whenever you turned away from that skunk. In this case, you might believe the spray of a skunk smells nice. You might pretend it smells nice over and over so many times, you forget you don't like it.

The process of creating beliefs that *go against your inner truth* is like that!

I knew people who lived close to a trash dump. They got so used to it, they didn't notice the retched smell in the air. That's another analogy for what it's like when we're conditioned to ignore how we feel. We get so used to ignoring our true feelings that we override how we feel because we don't even notice we are doing that.

Yet we can relearn to connect to how we feel and listen to our inner truth.

Truth-Telling Technique

Try this exercise. Take something you know is true, absolutely no doubt about it. For me, I love my children. That truth has no wiggle room, ever.

Now pick something that's 100 percent true for you. Close your eyes and state this truth out loud. Feel it in your body. Without working too hard, simply notice the state of your being. A "yes" feels like an opening and promotes an expansive feeling in my body.

Now make your statement false. Turn it around in such a way that it could *not* be true for you, but you state it as truth. In my example, my statement would be "I hate my children." When I close my eyes and say this, I feel a "no" sensation in my body. A "no" for me constricts my throat and tenses up my face.

Once you get in touch with noticing your body speak to you, you can check in with the truth of your body about anything. I do this when I grocery shop. My body lets me know what it wants to eat.

Many people to whom I've taught this technique said they couldn't feel anything at first. They couldn't hear or feel their body answer them. I know many of my clients don't feel safe in their bodies because of a history of physical abuse. When I ask them what they feel, their answers skip around the question, or they answer intellectually. That's okay. Those of us who aren't in touch with our inner truth or grounded in our body tend to have strong minds and intellectual ability. We think we have to figure out everything and live an effortful life.

However, with practice, intention, and patience, people will learn to feel their inner truth.

Connect With and Accept Your Inner Truth

How do you get in touch with your body's sensations? I would tell you to take a breath before you speak, to put your attention in your body and sense what's going on inside before talking. Taking a moment to ground yourself in your body and opening up your awareness makes a big difference in how you engage the moment. You want to change any habit into a conscious choice. With awareness you can do that. To connect to your inner truth of anger—to respond to life honorably, heroically, and powerfully—accept that having this kind of body awareness is necessary.

After connecting to your inner truth, the next step is to accept it. Your heart circulating blood through your body is an inner truth—one you can accept, of course. Your lungs breathing oxygen is another inner truth you accept as well. Your mouth creating saliva is a truth of your life with acceptance given, right? So when your body creates the sensation of anger, accept it as your inner truth, too.

As you learn to connect to your body and honor your truth with conscious choices, you might still want to defend your truth, your choice, your actions. I still feel compelled to defend my choices or how I feel sometimes. It's been a lifelong habit.

More often than not, though, I simply live my truth without judgment. There's no need to defend my choice or how I feel. Truth needs to only be accepted, not defended.

Imagine you're with a group of friends and have to pee. Your body has filtered the food and liquid you took in and needs to release it. Do you deny yourself and think, "Peeing is wrong, so I will ignore my full bladder." Or do you defend yourself to the group by saying, "Well, I know my bladder is doing its thing, and I really want to be with you. I'm so sorry to leave you. It's not that the bathroom is more important than you or I'm trying to escape your company." As ridiculous as this scenario sounds, I knew someone acted this way. It was true for her.

A woman I worked with in the corporate world had a belief that it wasn't okay to take care of herself while working. So one-hundred percent of her day at the office was working—nothing but working, doing stuff that her boss, colleagues, and customers wanted, and ignoring what she needed—including never peeing. Eventually, she had to be hospitalized with a severe infection caused by not taking pee breaks while at work. That's what so many of us do: We ignore our inner truth at our own peril.

TIME FOR YOUR TRUTH

To start, practice at least one minute of grounding. (See Introduction for Grounding Exercise instructions.) Then ask the following questions one at a time. Be curious and be gentle. After asking each question, close your eyes and *feel* into each answer.

Write down your answers and insights, taking special note of those that yield the strongest sensations in your body. I recommend answering them by speaking into a voice recorder on your smartphone or other device. You would review them while practicing Embodied Awareness. (See Introduction for instructions on Embodied Awareness.)

1) In what way do you override your truth? How do you know you are overriding your truth? How does that feel?
2) In what ways do you honor your inner truth? What does your inner truth feel like? How do you feel when you honor your truth?
3) Shadow self: What fears do you know you have that you choose to ignore? What emotions do you choose to deny, repress, or

judge? What qualities or aspects in others do you judge? And how might you be capable of that aspect or quality too?
4) How do you choose to unconsciously or consciously respond when you experience your own anger? Somebody else's?
5) What trauma or other experience has opened you up to or revealed a greater depth of self-truth?

SUGGESTED PRACTICE

Again, practice at least one minute of grounding and then take these actions:

- Make a commitment to honor a truth you've previously had difficulty honoring. The energy of commitment forms a contract with self and shifts something within you. A commitment highlights your truth barometer, which makes it more noticeable and uncomfortable if you override yourself. It creates more awareness to notice what your truth tells you in the moment.
- Be good enough for yourself, no matter what.
- Practice the Truth Telling Technique described in this chapter.
- Reflect on a situation that makes you angry. Feel the sensation of anger in your body, then breathe into that sensation.
  - State out loud: My inner truth of anger feels like (fill in the blank).
  - Breathe into the sensations.
  - State out loud: I acknowledge the energy of anger within me. I accept the energy of anger within me.
- Focus on your heart. Imagine breathing in and out through your heart space. Ask your heart, "How does my inner truth guide me to love myself?"
- Congratulate yourself for taking the time to connect to your inner truth.

Blaming Others

The World as Our Mirror

So many things piss us off. So many things make us despise one another. I'm pretty sure you are on somebody's shit list. I bet even I'm the cause of somebody's ire. And many of us get mad at ourselves. I hear and see people call themselves derogatory names often.

How many times a day do you hear someone blame somebody else? How often do you call yourself a name? Who do you blame and what do you blame them for?

Blame is a co-dependent pursuit. When victim mentality is part of your consciousness, it requires you to blame someone, resent someone, and have someone—anyone—be responsible for your happiness. But when you blame someone for your anger or lack of happiness, you give your power away. What happens?

When we give away our power, we de-value ourselves, our truth, and our worth. We de-appreciate ourselves, which gives rise to more anger. When it comes to connecting with your inner truth, blame is mutually exclusive. It keeps an unhappy, unfulfilling vicious circle going. And it keeps any solution out of reach.

 *Blame is disempowerment in action.*

Blame does not and cannot acknowledge the healthy emotional energy of anger. Remember the truth about anger: *It's a powerful natural energy that motivates change.* Its purpose is to help us grow into our life's vision with integrity. We compare it to an organically self-generated truth serum that informs our every decision as we interact with our world and grow into our future. Anger is a call to say "yes" to ourselves. Our inner truth of anger always has our back.

Biological Side of Anger

Anger has a biological component, too. As living organisms, healthy emotional energy helps us modulate our behavior. That's scientific lingo for saying that the healthy emotional energy of anger has helped our species survive and thrive.

Anger informs us by saying, "Based on what's going on in my life, I need to love myself in a specific way. I need my attention. What specifically do I need right now? What do I need to say 'yes' to? What do I need to say 'no' to?"

To answer these questions, we need to *feel* into them, and feeling into our healthy emotional energy of anger requires Embodied Awareness.

Embodied Awareness is the only way to connect to your inner truth and bring about change. If you're like me and have ignored, denied, or judged your inner truth for a long time, you'll require a committed, ongoing practice to create a new habit.

Embodied Awareness recognizes that your inner power is an inside job.

Each Person's Truth

How people feel relates to their experience, perception, and truth—each individual's truth. So when I was seven years old and my father punished me for stepping in mud puddles, it was *his* rage, not me, that caused him to violently strike me. His anger, experience, and perception caused his actions; I did not. He was reacting to his unconscious and subconscious habits, beliefs, and history. He had let being blind to his inner truth rule his life, violating me, my sisters, and especially himself.

When we lash out at people we care about, it's not their fault that our words and actions are hurtful. When we post on Facebook rants about who sucks, which politician is the devil, or what Facebook friend deserves to be unfriended, it's not about the other person. *It's always about us.* Calling people names or pointing fingers is a red flag indicating we're giving someone else the responsibility for our emotional wellbeing.

Life is filled with experiences of what's wrong with our world—and what's right. It's a continuum of powerless habits and conscious choices. Yet many of us operate from powerless habits while few of us make conscious choices.

Depending on which way you live in the moment, life can be somewhere between a vicious cycle and a profound transformation. For much of my life, I based my experiences on powerless habits that created a vicious cycle of victimization—until I learned I had a choice. Then I chose to create an honorable life based on the truth accessed through Embodied Awareness.

Responded Consciously

When I spoke to my children's father on Christmas Eve 1999, it was my experience, my perception, and my potential that created the healthy emotional energy of anger. It was my Embodied Awareness that allowed me to connect to my inner truth. Previously, in a similar situation, I would have ignored my inner truth of anger and given authority for my own wellbeing to the other person, squandering my empowered potential. I would have stayed on the phone and allowed myself to be the receiver of negative energy because I depended on the other for my happiness. However, when I hung up on my children's father that Christmas Eve, the healthy emotional energy of anger I felt made me respond *consciously*. My anger motivated change—that is, to honor myself with love and end the call.

That day, my anger moved me toward my vision of an honorable life. My anger asked me to say "yes" to me, and I listened. My inner truth truly became my source of inner power. When I'm connected to it, I know what to embrace and what to turn away.

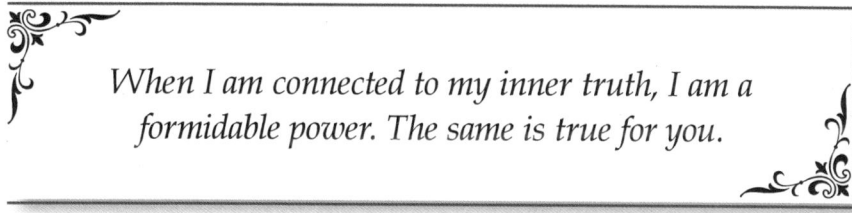

When I am connected to my inner truth, I am a formidable power. The same is true for you.

True power comes from within you. True power is free. True power is your trump card in the game of life. It's yours already and no one can ever take it away from you. But you can give it away through codependency–like I did for years.

Being Codependent

Since that Christmas Eve day, I admit, the old habit of codependency has tried to suck me in so I'd give away my power to someone else, making another responsible for my own fulfillment. I still diligently practice Embodied Awareness, and for sure, when I slip, it's easy for me to know because my discomfort tells me I'm looking outside of myself. I catch myself thinking "Who's fault is it for the way I feel?" That's a sure sign of being actively codependent.

In our culture, codependency is viral, and blame is common. We blame other people, the weather, animals, nature, aliens, and on and on. It's easy to point fingers blamefully when we aren't aware that *we* have the secret treasure within us.

Each of us has our own biology, brain, and individual expression of life—our own inner truth and potential. But we can't see opportunities for expanded potential if we're down in the muck of disempowered drama. When we zoom out and take a look with a higher awareness, we get a glimpse that "something more" is trying to happen. And the key to that "something more" dwells inside of us.

Imagine if we were to look at earth and its inhabitants from space, or squeeze all of it and us onto a microscope slide and examine it under an astronomically sized magnification. We'd look like identical organisms forming the building blocks of earthly life. All seven billion of us!

The First American Bitches

Idiots, jerks, and knuckleheads look the same as saints, superstars, and Samaritans. Bitches, too.

The first American bitches, the suffragettes, were blamed by those who opposed them for the anger these opponents experienced. The opposition pointed fingers at these women, calling them contemptible, mean, and offensive. They externalized their anger, and that's exactly what blame does. Acting violently toward these first American bitches, they somehow rationalized their actions by their fears, their anger, and their lack of awareness.

But the suffragettes (aka bitches) weren't about blame. Instead, they allowed their own anger to motivate change through peaceful measures, and they succeeded. They did not give away their power to the oppressors. They continued to picket, speak out, and give lectures. They kept asking themselves and members of their groups—American

ANGER 101

Women Suffragette Organization and National American Woman Suffrage Association—this question: "What more can we do?"

These heroic, honorable, and powerful women were relentless in creating change and equality. The opposition had already tried to take away women's power through legislation and force. But nothing could suppress these courageous women's inner truth.

In the end, they created a new empowered beginning for women in 1920 when the nineteenth amendment to the U.S. Constitution was passed. Looking back at the levels of awareness in mass consciousness and the oppression that existed, I feel awe and admiration for the heroism, honor, and power these first American bitches embodied. They showed us a universal truth—a grand potential—as well as the ability to harmoniously create a different world, even when times are dark.

Whether we like it or not, we're all responsible for life as it's expressed through our shared humanity while hurling through space at a thousand miles an hour.

Each time we label another person, place, or thing with a derogatory name, we squander a measure of our authentic power. Each time we place blame on another, we make ourselves a victim of circumstance. Each time we blame someone for a life we don't enjoy, we create a further separation between ourselves and our hearts' desire.

> *Name-calling and blame support the structures that keep polarity, separation, and oppression alive.*

Each time we externalize an experience and look to another to make a change for the better, we weaken and dishonor our inherent wisdom, our power. And at a thousand miles an hour, that makes us go nowhere fast. Or at least nowhere we want to be.

Held Captive

In addition, when we give another credit for creating a world we don't like, we are held captive in a prison of our own making. When we are actively codependent in a world where blame, intolerance, and violence are status quo, the obvious way to create change is not so obvious. When we externalize our pain, our sorrow, our disdain, our anger—rather than acknowledge the inner workings of this truth—we invest our energy into creating more external factors that make us think, "It's all about the other person."

If we ignore our inner truth, we have seven billion others who will help highlight it. And highlight they will—until that inner truth has been acknowledged.

The archetype of the pointing fingers is the archetype of a disempowered life defined by victimhood, external stimuli, and disassociation from your inner truth. An empowered life is fueled by your internal wisdom, conscious choice, and authentic power—whether you're a housewife, a president, or an author.

> *Of all the infinite sources of power in the world, the most transformative power is the one within.*

A Transformative Power

Your inner power can transform you through a process that doesn't get much hoopla in schools, media, or other institutions. It's this: When someone ruffles your feathers, use the experience to transform your life. It's an authentically powerful process, simple but not easy, yet it can actually transform the world—I swear my life on it.

Here's how to tap into that power:

ANGER 101

1) Be curious about what you are feeling when you experience a reaction of disdain, anger, disgust, hate, ire.
2) Instead of immediately judging and resisting the experience or the person who got your attention, accept that the moment exists just as it is.
3) In a spirit of curiosity and acceptance, shift your awareness on that "outside" event by focusing your attention on what you feel "inside."
4) Notice any sensations and where in your body you feel them. Stay with each one and simply notice it as if you were looking at a folded up t-shirt. "Oh, there it is."
5) Feel into the sensations of YOU and ask yourself these questions: What in your life needs your attention? How can you love yourself more in each moment?
6) Honor the answers that come to you. Honor YOU. Take action if needed.
7) With self-acknowledgment, self-honor, and self-love, as you use this transformative process, give thanks to the "outer" experience for leading you home to what needs you most: YOU.

If this process sounds stupid and you're thinking, "That women is (fill in the blank with a negative word) and wasting my time," here's an opportunity. Again, when something *outside of you* disturbs you (in this case, me and my process), take it as a cue that something *inside of you* wants attention. Consider the cause and effect of the conflict residing within. It's causing the disturbing experience outside of you rather than the other way around. You see, the world is your mirror.

Look, I'm serious. If I (or somebody else) pisses you off, I'm doing you a favor. The more enraged you get, the bigger the potential exists for you. This opportunity can help you reclaim your power and create a world you prefer. But you must start from the inside out. If you ignore your internal world, life will give you countless opportunities to oppose something or someone.

> *If you continue to blame something or someone for driving you crazy, you'll be pointing arthritic fingers until you're six feet under.*

Externalizing Anger

Many people externalize their anger. It started for me as a child. I clearly saw and experienced when my father, my step-father, and my first partner externalized their anger onto me.

Specifically, they blamed me for the overpowering discomfort with life they experienced. They blamed me for doing what they did to themselves. My father was disconnected from his inner truth; he did not listen to his inherent wisdom. He also was conditioned to strike out at his children for simply being children—an unconscious repeat from his childhood when he'd been beat up by his father. So when I just did normal little girl stuff, my dad was triggered by unacknowledged, long-held emotions. He perceived that I didn't listen to him, so he reacted unconsciously with violence toward me. That's what he was taught and had experienced himself.

When we make a habit of being disconnected with our inner truth, the pressure builds and seeks release. The thing is, with a habit of disconnection from the inner truth of anger, we will either externalize our anger or turn it inward. Neither action is acknowledging or honorable.

Unconscious *action* does nothing to assuage the inner truth of anger or dissipate the pressure. Unconscious *reaction* continues the negative habit of disassociating with our inherent wisdom. That's why people who are mean, aggressive, or violent continue that bullying behavior with themselves as well as others.

> *When you deny your inner truth, no action on the outside can honor your inner truth, so the energy remains stagnate, always building and seeking release.*

I often see externalized anger in the public eye and on Facebook. I can identify who in the news and online are disconnected from their inner truth. They're unaware of what they need in order to assuage the wounding within. I feel their needy energy and see it in their actions and words—without judgment. Yes, I can see it with clarity. And as an empathic person, I can feel it, too.

Take, for instance, what really bothers you. I mean what *really* bothers you—so much that you feel stressed. If it's a person, you might call that person a name or blame that person for atrocities that go against your values. You might give that person unsolicited advice or try to fix him or her.

Consider this explanation: Whatever that person is doing, saying, or experiencing, it triggers in you an unmet need, an inner truth that's been ignored. It relates to something about what you do to yourself or what has been done to you that hasn't been acknowledged. It comes alive through the other's experience. That unacknowledged need or disassociated part of self can be called the shadow—something you project onto others when you don't accept it in yourself. And that non-acceptance means you're also judging yourself.

> *When we judge ourselves, we cannot, absolutely can not, have inner peace. We cannot be authentically powerful.*

If we build a hundred charitable endeavors that operate 24/7 to address the problems on our planet, or if we build a hundred schools to train superheroes to save the world yet ignore our internal sensations when they get triggered, we keep those endeavors and demand to build a million more.

Changing one's life is not a one-sided effort. Yes, take action steps on the outside and also on the inside. Let's deeply acknowledge what is happening within, that part of us that's our home, our life, our power. When we do, the power of our conscious choice ripples out into the world with a force to heal dissonance. And it starts with our own selves.

> *Oh yes, we must be the change we want to see.*
> *To do otherwise is to be part of the problem.*

A Divine Miracle

When you judge yourself, disconnect from your inner truth, or externalize your anger, you generate more discomfort and lack of fulfillment in your life. The key is in *knowing* you are a miracle. You are divine. You have a right to how you feel. And in any given moment, how you feel is a truth of your existence in that moment. It is your inherent and unique inner wisdom.

By comparison, when you cut off a part of yourself in judgment or disassociation, you disempower yourself. Instead, turn disempowerment and lack of awareness into empowerment and Embodied Awareness.

Instead of pointing fingers of blame, open your life to the power that will transform your world.

Instead of judging yourself, start loving yourself and accepting however you feel, what you think, and who you are. No judging.

The world starts within you, not the other way around. The inner truth of your existence in any given situation will set you free. A breath of awareness and conscious choice expands your inner peace, and you also bless the world with the same. You'll find that the inner peace you've blessed yourself with is reflected in your outside world—like a mirror.

Falling Back

As aware as I'd become, I found myself falling into old subconscious habits when I met Rod at a community gathering. He was handsome, artistic, and lived closed by. What's more, he was single. So before long, he and I started dating.

But within a month, I felt discomfort with our new relationship. No matter how beautiful I looked, I didn't get acknowledged by him. No matter what gifts I presented him, I didn't receive a thank you. When I scrubbed his dirty bathroom and later helped him host a party, I didn't even get a kiss. My heart dropped.

Yes, I felt the healthy emotional energy of anger. But I reacted with an old way of being: ignore what was going on inside of me, be painfully and passively silent, and judge myself. "Lori what's wrong with you?" "Why do you have to be so damn picky?" "You're afraid of committing to a relationship, so you'd better make this one work."

Yet, experience after experience with Rod left me feeling unhappy. Finally, a year after it began, I woke up. I knew I was attractive, and *I was not the reason* Rod showed me no physical affection. I was worthy of love, and *I was not the reason* Rod didn't want to make love to me. Nor was the problem I was afraid of commitment. Rod and I simply didn't share the same relationship values. Why would I stay in a relationship that didn't work for me? So I ended it.

My relationship with Rod turned into a blessing because it once again pushed me to seek support. In my coaching, I saw how I was judging myself for not being fulfilled and blaming Rod for not meeting my needs. Each time during the year when I felt the sensation of my heart dropping, I had immediately disassociated with my body and my inner truth. I popped into my head and judged myself for being wrong in some way. His inability to love and appreciate me mirrored how I wasn't loving or appreciating myself. I was the one not meeting my needs.

The thing is, the first time I felt this dropping sensation with Rod, my inner truth of anger was telling me, "Nope. No thank you. Lori, it ain't gonna work with this guy. He won't fulfill the vision you have of a romantic relationship. Say goodbye to that guy, will ya?" Instead, when I'd feel my heart drop, the old pattern whispered, "Suck it up, Lori. Something's wrong with you. Try harder." Had I heeded the guidance of my inner truth, I would have ended the relationship within the first two weeks instead of a year later—and cried a lot fewer tears.

Here's what I've come to know: All along, Rod was who he was. Yes, for the first few weeks excitement and hormones let him be loving and affectionate, but those initial responses stopped quickly. Still I believed he could be what I wanted him to be, yet I refused to see him as *who he was*.

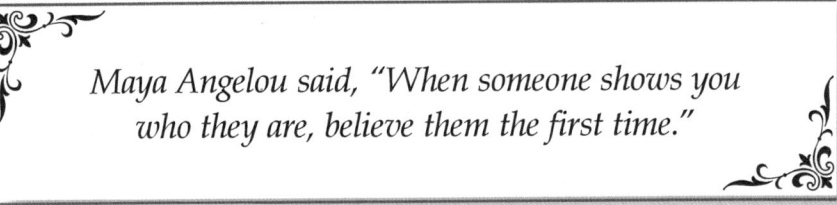

Maya Angelou said, "When someone shows you who they are, believe them the first time."

My inner truth agrees with Maya, but my old habits and conditioning responded otherwise. I blamed him and judged myself. Ultimately, Rod mirrored how I treated myself.

TIME FOR YOUR TRUTH

To start, practice at least one minute of grounding. (See Introduction for Grounding Exercise instructions.) Then ask the following questions one at a time. Be curious and be gentle. After asking each question, close your eyes and *feel* into each answer.

Write down your answers and insights, taking special note of those that yield the strongest sensations in your body. I recommend answering them by speaking into a voice recorder on your smartphone or other device. You would review them while practicing Embodied Awareness. (See Introduction for instructions on Embodied Awareness.)

1) Who or what do you find yourself blaming for anything? What do you blame them for? What qualities or lack of qualities does the object of your blame have?
2) How often do you lash out at others or call them derogatory names? When do you do that?
3) How often do others lash out at you or call you derogatory names? When does that happen?
4) Based on what's going on in your life right now, what is asking for your attention?
5) Have you ever considered you can transform blame by being heroic, honorable, and powerful for yourself? What are your thoughts about this? Your feelings?

SUGGESTED PRACTICE

Again, practice at least one minute of grounding and then take these actions:

- Create a list of statements that are 100% true for you. Then create a list of statements that are 100% false. Throughout the week, practice Embodied Awareness and learn how your body

expresses "yes" and "no." Become familiar with the wisdom of your body in this way.
- Reflect on a situation that makes you angry. (Choose from Time For Your Truth above number 1, 2, 3, or 4.) Feel the sensation of anger in your body. Breathe into that sensation.
    o State out loud: *My inner truth of anger feels like (fill in the blank).*
    o Breathe into the sensations.
    o State out loud: *I acknowledge the energy of anger within me. I accept the energy of anger within me.*
    o *** Ask your inner truth: *How does my inner truth guide me to love myself? What changes do I need to make?*
- Choose an inspired action based on *** above and commit to being heroic, honorable, and powerful for yourself this week.
- Congratulate yourself for taking the time to connect to your inner truth!

Love That Moves Mountains

The Fall to Freedom

Recently I was in a romantic relationship with a wonderful man. Eric and I met at a five-day spiritual intensive. After the intensive ended, we stayed in touch and soon learned we shared many values. In fact, we were a lot alike. So much of what made me different than most people I know made me similar to him, which made me excited to get to know Eric.

I had started to get my home ready for sale earlier that year, about four months before the intensive. It took a lot of work and emotions to prepare the estate, my home and sanctuary for twenty-two years. I sold, donated, or gave away more than ninety-five percent of my worldly possessions.

I had shared this house with my two children for their entire lives, as well as our dog, and three cats. Also, my father had lived with me for a few years and my mother had died in this home.

Letting go of everything took about a year. Yet this goodbye to my old life was even bigger because I was leaving long-established relationships in Pennsylvania and moving across the country. In the midst of it all, I took time for the intensive so I could be with a group of heart-centered people. I sensed they could offer me a huge dose of unconditional love and support that would carry me through the rest of the year.

At the end of that year, just three weeks before I journeyed to my new home in the southwest, I joined my two children in Europe for winter holidays. I cherished my time with them and yet, being on the go in Paris, touring the countryside, and visiting friends in Belgium had me seriously considering if I'd lost my marbles. Feeling exhausted when I arrived in France, I was almost debilitated by the time I returned to Pennsylvania. I gave myself only four days to finish packing, get the pets ready for their cross-country pet transport, hold a ceremony to say goodbye to the old place, and then board the plane and fly to Arizona. By the time I arrived in Tucson, I was emotionally, physically, and mentally bankrupt. It was January 8th, 2016.

Trying to invest in a long-distance romantic relationship during such a tumultuous time might seem ridiculous, but I was so immersed in transformation and change that adding one more huge life experience to the hurricane didn't seem out of place. Indeed, because of this emotional whirlwind, having Eric's support and love felt great. Many times his presence felt like the calm in middle of the storm.

Eric lived closer to Arizona than Pennsylvania but in another state, which meant one of us would have to travel to see each other. At first, it was he who did the traveling, but when he visited me, having a houseguest in my new house in an unknown city felt draining.

Still, his desire to be with me in person or on Facetime grew with each passing day. That happens in a normal growing relationship. Yet my desire to sleep, restore, root, rest, and even hide grew each day. In fact, my exhaustion left me with little strength and embodied awareness. I was anything but normal during this time. My body was numb. My mind was weak. My emotions were all over the place. Because he is a beautiful man inside and out, I made the effort to give him all I could. The truth was, though, it represented an enormous effort for me. I didn't have anything to give that wouldn't bankrupt me even further.

Looking back, how I pushed it for so long is a testament to how powerful the fears and false beliefs of my subconscious were. Considering the shell of a woman I had become, it felt to me I was going beyond the call of duty. But for Eric, my efforts weren't enough. That revealed another old pattern in my life; no matter what effort I made, I was never giving or being enough for the significant man in my life. At least it felt that way.

Resentment built within me, but my old habit of overriding how I felt pulled stronger. I said "yes" to him and "no" to me—again and again.

My being in this relationship didn't flow. I'd feel the familiar pang in my chest when he expected more from me or when I sensed his disappointment about my level of engagement. Yes, I'd notice the sensation but then I'd push it into the periphery of my experience until I forgot about it. I became good at ignoring what I needed and being afraid of expressing my own needs. I had learned the ways of the silent child almost as soon as I was born. I had also learned how to exchange my inner truth for a painful passive silence, just as my mother had modeled. In my weakened state, these ways re-emerged with strength.

Surprised This Pattern Showed Up Again

Having this old relationship pattern still alive within me surprised me. I knew that from having a relationship with David the year before I moved to Arizona. The old pattern didn't work with him.

David was a person who didn't ask me for more than I could give. Incredibly attentive and thoughtful, he looked after me, probably saying "yes" to me more than I said "yes" to him. I found my time with David very healing. It convinced me my old habit of "not being enough" was over. So I was surprised that, with Eric, I resurrected this old habit and let it follow me.

So here I was in a new land in desperate need for TLC. I needed my own mega-attention as I recovered from my big move. Big transitions require gentleness and patience. I had been coached on that the previous year, and I coached my clients on that.

Yet here was the biggest transition in my life and I was making someone else more important than me. I was missing the people I loved. I was grieving. Everything was new. The only familiar thing was a revived subconscious pattern of making myself wrong and the other person right.

In May 2016, though, everything changed again.

For no logical reason, I had felt called to Tucson—a strong, clear call powerful enough for me to sell my family home, let go of almost everything in my life, and leave the people I loved. I had questioned myself while friends and family questioned me. And though I didn't have an answer that made sense, I had known I needed to move there.

It wasn't until I climbed Mt. Lemmon near the city of Tucson that I got a hint of the mystery that called me here. Eric and I had climbed Mt. Lemmon together in February. A strenuous hike, we had to climb over boulders, avoid open abandoned mines, protect ourselves from the cacti, gravel, heat, and watch out for dangerous wild things that lived in the desert. But despite the obvious challenges, nothing could prevent me from heeding the call of the mountain. I felt pulled to the cliff face.

We hiked for about an hour till we got to a magical area—a place in which a magnetic vortex of energy drew me in. For a few minutes, I stood about fifty feet from the foot of the cliff face and looked up feeling a fire surging within me.

"Eric, I need to get up there. Now." I started moving up quickly as if my feet didn't touch the ground. In a few breaths, I reached the top and immediately embraced the large wall of rock to merge as one.

I am not exaggerating when I call that mountain a portal. What I experienced was supernatural. There, hugging the cliff face, I was swallowed into the belly of the ancients who, it seemed, had eagerly waited for me for thousands of years.

That day was a homecoming in which I felt love in that mountain like I had never felt before. The mountain embraced me as I stretched out my arms and leaned into the flat hard rock. I could hear the mountain speak to me. I could feel it embrace me. Though my intellect didn't appreciate the mystical experience and wanted to call me foolish, my ego could not argue away this experience. Immediately, I knew who had invited me to Tucson as if I never needed to go anywhere else. *I belonged there.*

Those ancient beings are a part of me, as I am them. We are of the same essence.

Second Trip to the Mountain

Naturally after the first trip to the mountain, I was eager to return. On Friday, May 13th—almost four months after the first visit—it was time. I was being asked to come, and I needed to go for the love and support that awaited me. My logical brain could make no sense of what I was asked to do, but my heart needed no explanation. It was saying, "Go Lori. Nothing else is more real than this connection. Go." So I went.

This time, I traveled alone. The hike up the mountain takes physical effort and stamina, but it felt natural to me—a strong, athletic, adventurous woman. Confident in my physical abilities, I trusted I'd be protected in this sacred place. My backpack carried a hearty lunch and plenty of water plus ceremonial items that would allow the mystery of life to flow *from* me and *into* me through sacred veneration.

Half way up the mountain, I stopped and sat for a while under a mesquite tree, taking time for a cold drink and a snack. I leaned up against a boulder in the shade for thirty minutes and enjoyed the view, feeling both patience and anticipation as I looked up toward my destination.

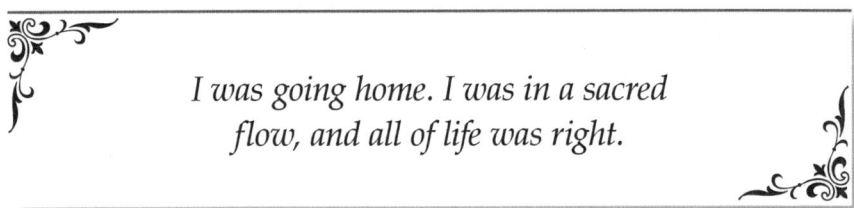

I was going home. I was in a sacred flow, and all of life was right.

Starting back up the mountain, I could feel that magnetic pull again. This time, my climb was more deliberate. I felt my feet touch the earth with each reverent step. My rhythmic breathing sounded along with the crunch of my boots against the dry desert ground. I felt so safe, so loved, and so at home—perfection.

The place I had visited with Eric in February loomed before me, and in another ten minutes of climbing, I found an intimate place among the ancients. A large boulder provided a throne and the rock face supported my back. There, I felt solid and majestic as I took in views of the surrounding peaks and valleys. Indeed, I was the only living creature I could see or hear other than a hawk's screech overhead.

In that place, I opened myself up to the intimacy of the mountain beings, and they communicated with me as I celebrated my return with lunch and a sacred ritual. Three hours later, I wasn't ready to leave, but I knew it was smart to return to the car before sunset. I packed up and set off down the mountain.

About twenty paces down, I stepped onto a boulder as I'd done many times before. But unlike those other times, this boulder moved, and I moved with it. In an unlikely and shocking instant, I pummeled down the side of the mountain in a traumatic bouncing roll from one boulder to the next. Fast and furiously, I tumbled, rolled, and bounced—a violent fall. I tried to grab onto something to slow or stop the fall, but I was quickly convinced the power of the mountain was in control. Fear didn't exist. My mind and body submitted to the force of gravity. *I became surrender.*

Eventually, the flat top of a boulder stopped the fierce momentum of the fall. I landed on my back with my body splayed out in all directions.

I lay still on the boulder and crevice mountainside. The shock of the descent vibrated within my traumatized body. I could feel both a numbness and aliveness throughout my physical and emotional being. And pain. Lots of pain.

I lifted my head to survey my body, examining my limbs and feeling relieved I could move them, if only slightly. I should have been relieved my back wasn't broken, but that thought didn't cross my mind. My right shin was bleeding, swelling up purple through the tear in my hiking pants. My right forearm was scraped raw and full of deep scratches. I felt trickles of blood on my face. An egg-sized bump protruded on the left crown of my head. And the biggest injury occurred to my left thigh—a hard solid mound of inflammation. I felt numbing and pain along the outside of my thigh from my knee to my hip. But no broken bones.

A Great Curiosity

Although in shock, I also had a great curiosity. What in the world just happened? I was in sacred reverence with ancient beings who embraced me and communicated with me, and I was an adept hiker. I felt no anger, no resentment—just curiosity. My body had lots of pain. My intellect was eager to get busy and do something. I had a little bit of ice in my lunch bag. My backpack, still strapped on, was stretched out by my left shoulder. I squirmed out of it in slow motion.

Sitting up challenged my will but I succeeded. Then I put the baggie of melting ice on my injured shin and lay back down. I'd let the ice sit on my shin for at least ten minutes or until it melted completely. Mostly, I needed my legs to work so I could climb down the rest of the mountain, which was still *most* of the mountain. The sun was low in the west shining hot and bright. If I could get up and walk to the car before sunset, then my safety was in no further jeopardy, I thought.

I stayed another fifteen minutes before trying to stand up. Still filled with wonderment and curiosity, surprisingly I didn't cry. I had never before fallen so severely. I had never been that bruised and physically traumatized so immediately. Even the whiplash from the automobile accident that inspired this book was gentler in its injury to me.

It was hard to imagine how I'd make it down the mountain alone, in the heat, with both of my legs injured. My left leg felt like a piece of solid lumber stiffer than any body part had been before. Somehow I stood up. But I knew my strength. And I knew I had to get down to my car.

I gently, slowly moved my rigid and aching body. After squirming back into my backpack, I looked up at the mountain face and received silence. Nothing was offered. So I turned and looked down the mountain, took a deep breath, said a prayer, and took my first step.

A painful descent put me back at the car at the last light of the day. I moaned my way into the front seat and drove home. That night, I soaked in an Epsom salt bath and went to bed earlier than usual. The next morning after breakfast, all I was capable of was another Epsom salt soak and then back to bed. I allowed myself to stay in bed all day, floating in and out of sleep. Since the left side of my body could bear no weight, I lay on my right side.

That afternoon when I woke up, I checked my phone and saw several messages from Eric. I texted him to let him know I was resting. He told me he was worried I might have a concussion. Was it my insecurities or his discontent that told me I should be more attentive to our relationship? Yet the only thing I was capable of was providing the TLC my body screamed for. No way could I ignore the inner truth of my traumatized body. Any subconscious beliefs and relationship patterns were no match for this physical trauma!

Along with the physical pain came a healthy dose of anger telling me I needed *me*. And as only anger can do, it shouted at me to establish tighter boundaries in my relationship with Eric—to say "yes" to myself once and for all.

The Gift of the Fall

Later that week was when I realized the true gift of my fall. I had been ignoring my inner truth in this new relationship. Again and again, I said "yes" to Eric and "no" to me. Throughout our short-lived romantic relationship, the sensations of anger in my chest rose up to say, "No, that doesn't work for me." But instead I'd say, "Okay, sure."

Over and again, I felt the need to defend my actions, my decisions, my life. Then after the fall, the only "yes" that was possible was a "yes" for me, for my life. Naturally Eric wanted time and attention, if only to let him know I was okay. But my aching, bruised body needed *my* time and attention more. In effect, the seriousness of my physical condition highlighted my inner and outer truth—that my needs stood as tall as the mountain.

For the first time in my relationship with Eric, I honored what I needed. The power of the mountain knew that the only way to the summit of my personal power was to heed the call of my majesty once and for all. My connection to the ancients was a love that moved mountains. And because of it, I fell to freedom.

Saying "Yes" to Me

In the days that followed, I found the words to let Eric know what was going on for me—what had been going on since the end of the previous year. I needed to give *only me* what I needed until I could root in my new home, in my new life. Added to that was time to heal from the fall. Being the man he is, Eric understood that heeding the call of my inner voice was the blessing made obvious from the fall. So he didn't press me for more. When I stood in my truth, he listened.

Only when we honor ourselves can others honor us back.

Surrendering to Self-honor

The power of saying "yes" to *me* in this relationship was mostly complete within three days. However, healing my physical body took more than four months. As I write at the end of 2016, a few small areas of injured tissue remain in my left thigh. It's there reminding me to make a surrendering to self-honor a natural practice.

This experience was not about the man I was in relationship with, though Eric is wonderful. Rather, it was about my inability to say "yes" to myself and go against a childhood pattern. The consequences of this fall down the mountain almost had nothing to do with him, and yet they did. He had held such an unconditional loving space for me that when I started to say "yes" to myself, he heard and supported me. I felt safe with him.

Now I know that when I honor me and give myself what I need, no one expects me to do anything differently.

For all of us, the most powerful, fulfilling life is lived by honoring our inner truth. So let's fall in love with saying "yes" to ourselves.

The Value of Trauma

Traumatic experiences like my fall down the mountain can wake up a person to a greater truth. Traumatic experiences can also reflect a pattern. We might learn early on that life is traumatic, so our subconscious continues to create trauma.

Increasing awareness can come through gentleness at times. But to accomplish gentle learning requires a conscious choice and commitment to be made. It's too easy to fall back into the same old patterns. With awareness, commitment, and conscious choice, we can slowly create new habits that will replace old ones.

Embodied Awareness gives power to our conscious choices and energy shifts. It allows us to choose and follow new habits such as listening to the inner truth of anger and saying "yes" to ourselves.

Trauma is not a requirement to learn this, but it's often the catalyst. Falling down a mountain to attain freedom from limiting beliefs became my catalyst. Until then, my steadfast commitment to self-love had competed with an old habit based on fear and conditioning. That's how the mountain helped me fall to freedom.

TIME FOR YOUR TRUTH

To start, practice at least one minute of grounding. (See Introduction for Grounding Exercise instructions.) Then ask the following questions one at a time. Be curious and be gentle. After asking each question, close your eyes and *feel* into each answer.

Write down your answers and insights, taking special note of those that yield the strongest sensations in your body. I recommend answering them by speaking into a voice recorder on your smartphone or other device. You would review them while practicing Embodied Awareness. (See Introduction for instructions on Embodied Awareness.)

1) What's one thing you know is true for you but you've been ignoring? What's one thing you dread but have the power to change?
2) Consider one area of your life in which you know an old habit needs to be replaced with a more fulfilling choice. What wants to happen? What is this experience asking you to be? To do?
3) What challenging experience in your life has led to more freedom, to more truth?
4) Consider an illness or injury that you experienced. Shift your perception of the illness or injury from being an inconvenience to insight about inner wisdom. What would that insight be? What is its message?
5) Have you experienced a supernatural, transpersonal, or mystical event? What was your perception of it? What was its meaning in your life? Did it have a practical application?

SUGGESTED PRACTICE

Again, practice at least one minute of grounding and then take these actions:

- Practice Embodied Awareness and the Acknowledgment Cycle to tap into inner wisdom for Time For Your Truth number 2 in the list above. Choose an inspired action and carry it out.
- Give yourself TLC this week, just because.
- Reflect on something this week that created the healthy emotional energy of anger for you. As you do, practice the Acknowledgment Cycle.
- Celebrate your commitment to yourself.

Letting Go

Surrender to the Moment

Shortly after I arrived in Tucson, I tried sensory deprivation therapy. It involves a large enclosed holding tank filled with water about ten inches deep and eight hundred pounds of Epsom salt. People get in the tank, close the door, and float.

You may be wondering why they would voluntarily enclose themselves in a claustrophobic salty environment and float in water that many strangers had been in previously. Yes, it sounds weird, but my research on the health benefits of floating produced rave reviews so I thought, "Why not?" I wanted to support myself however I could, and with *everything* being new in my home, I was willing to try this new therapy.

So far, I've floated three times in 2016 and have one more on the books for 2017. Here's what happens.

First, I take the required shower before entering the flotation chamber. Then I insert ear plugs. (The first time I floated, I didn't wear earplugs. Mistake. For the next week 24/7, loud cracking audio played in my eardrums louder than any earwax experience of my life. Lesson learned.) Floating is swimsuit optional, so I float naked. After entering the tank, I close the door and I'm sealed into a private womb of darkness.

There's an immense trust required to shut yourself off to the rest of the world in a tiny chamber without access to technology or another human. At least that's the way it feels for me. For a few minutes, a quiet music plays in the tank as I get settled into the hour-long soak. I lie down, center my long body in the middle of the tank, let my arms find natural floating positions, and let go. Flotation time begins.

It's amazing how loud and annoying my mind is when I'm deprived of stimulation and when nothing is required of me. I wonder how I will just lie there for a full hour doing nothing. Why am I doing this? Will this time go fast? What if I don't hear the music come back on telling me the hour is up? What if someone comes in the room and steals my clothes, my jewelry, my purse? Can I do flotation wrong? Is there enough oxygen in this thing?

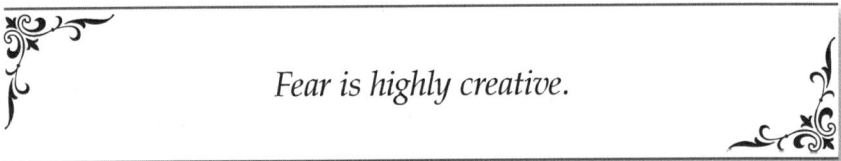

Fear is highly creative.

I detach from the meanderings of infinite thoughts by putting awareness in my body—a floating kind of awareness. I notice where I'm holding tension. At first, I become aware that my neck is trying to keep my head above water. With eight hundred pounds of Epsom salt, there is no way my head or any part of me will sink, so I intentionally release my neck muscles.

There's nothing I need to do to float. No effort required. Yet within moments, my neck starts to tense up again. Again, I release. Then I feel the crown of my head tilting up as if it's trying to trick me into believing it's really not "doing" anything. I allow gravity to pull my head back into the water, then I check my limbs to make sure they are heavy in the water. I repeat, "There's nothing you need to do, Lori."

In the darkness, there is nothing to see. Although I open and close my eyes a bunch of times, the darkness looks the same either way. That's when I decide darkness is more comfortable with my eyes closed. The longer I float, the more I become aware of all the ways my body is trying to work at doing something, anything, and it's usually something completely unnecessary.

I scan my body trying to catch myself making an effort to be more float-worthy. When I find an area of my body trying to take control, I release a little more. Every now and again I think, "Oh my god, this is going to seem like I'm in here forever." I add a few prayers. Hum a little. Think some more. Scan some more.

I realize I'm driving myself crazy, so I make a conscious choice to let go and accept myself with all my struggle, control, fear. Everything.

Then it happens: I hear the music come back on, alerting me my hour is over. It's then I realize that somewhere during that hour of quietly freaking out, I've let go of all the thinking and replaced it with a state of sublime do-nothing being-ness. An effortless salty utopia.

I open the door. Everything is still as I left it, I see. So I crawl out, take a shower, get dressed, and leave.

Surrender to the Moment

Letting go and surrendering to the moment is much like the experience in the flotation tank. Often we think we must do something to prove ourselves worthy. But like in the flotation tank, we need not do *anything* to be float-worthy; *we just are*. There's nothing to control. Fear is creative in or outside the flotation tank, and when we feel ourselves tense up, we can simply breathe and release.

Just like the eight hundred pounds of Epsom salt, life will support us if we let it.

Effort is a habit. Struggle is a habit. These days, I'm highly aware of what's going on in my body. I can feel when my body starts to tense up in the slightest way. It happens when I have a fleeting thought of fear for some future thing, or when I'm judging myself, or when I think I should be doing this when I'm doing that.

Sometimes when I'm feeling sadness, anger, grief, or depression, tension comes the second I think I should not be feeling that way. I notice quickly. But when I open up to the perfection of the moment, accept it as it is—*as I am*—whatever I initially resisted has transformed. The music of life comes on, and the next moment presents itself. I didn't have to do anything.

It's amazing how powerful the moment is when we accept how we feel and allow ourselves to be just as we are. To not accept ourselves is a disassociation from the moment and judgment of self—not an easy, honorable, or grace-filled experience.

Accepting *how I am* is the biggest surrender. My body relaxes when I allow that—just being me with no expectations. Letting go, surrendering, and accepting makes the moment simpler, and the simpler I make my moments, the more powerful they become.

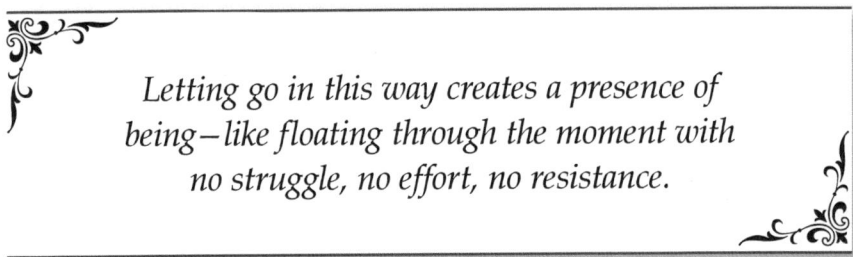

Letting go in this way creates a presence of being—like floating through the moment with no struggle, no effort, no resistance.

Uganda Trip

In 2003, I took my second trip to the primary school in Uganda where I helped out in the year 2000. I was flying Ethiopian Airlines out of Newark, New Jersey. My Ugandan friend Martha drove me, my carry on, and two huge suitcases to the airport. One suitcase was filled with donated books and the other with household donations and school

ANGER 101

supplies. Thankfully, everything fit comfortably in my Audi A6 station wagon.

My car should have provided a quality ride, but a piece of it under the front bumper had a habit of falling off—and it did so along the New Jersey turnpike. (Audi has since remedied this defect, but what a pain it was for a few years.) Along the highway a few miles from the airport, that front piece started dragging on the pavement. We pulled over so I could fix it, but crawling under my Audi on the New Jersey turnpike stressed me. I shoved the piece back in place and then pounded on it to snap it in as hundreds of cars raced by. With that temporarily remedied, I got back in the car with dirty hands and crunchy knees. What a way to start a day-and-a-half journey to Uganda!

When we arrived at Newark Airport, we parked so Martha could help me with the heavy luggage. We entered the Ethiopian Airlines check-in area and saw the business class check-in on the left and the crowded coach class section on the right. I held a coach class ticket but decided to stand in the business line. The previous year around the same time of the summer, I had traveled to Uganda on Ethiopian Airlines and got upgraded to business class for $400 one way. That made a very long journey more comfortable. Besides, I had more room to stretch out and sleep as well as better food, better service, and personal hygienic amenities. In addition, the luggage allowance for business class allowed two check-in pieces compared one in coach. In coach class, additional bags cost $150 apiece. Business class ticket holders were also given more generous standards for luggage allowance than coach. "A kilo over? No problem. We'll take care of that for you."

Typically the last thing you want to experience (but I have many times) is getting to the check-in counter and finding out your luggage is overweight. Right there, in front of impatient eyes standing in a curving line behind you, you have to unpack your undies and everything else, redistribute the weight, and decide what precious cargo isn't that precious so you can meet the weight limit. The curving line of eyes watch. They know; they've had to do it before, too. Especially if you fly coach to a developing country, you know this process. In my experience, flying business class eliminates this risk.

The business class line was much shorter than the adjoining coach class line at check-in because the business class cabin has fewer seats. Still, the line was moving slow, so slow it took the same amount of time for the ten people in front of me to go through check-in as it did for dozens of people in coach to go through. Feeling annoyed, I still felt smug knowing that, by upgrading to business class, I wouldn't have to go through the unpleasant ordeal of unpacking. However, the clock showed me I was pushing the time before my flight departed. "I need this line to move."

Finally, it was my turn. Martha walked with me to the check-in counter while dragging the large heavy black duffel. "Hi, I'm flying to Uganda on flight 847 and would like to upgrade to business class, please." I handed the agent my passport.

The Ethiopian Airlines agent took my passport and typed away on her computer keyboard, then asked, "Have you requested the upgrade already? I don't see it in the system."

"No, I haven't. Last year I did it at the time of check in."

"I'm sorry to say that there are no upgrades available. Business class is full."

My heart and shoulders dropped. Gravity added another hundred pounds to my body. Then I glanced over to the coach line. It was so long, it snaked out the door. Would I miss my flight?

"Uhm. What should I do? My flight leaves soon. Are you sure? I have two check-in bags, and the coach class line is out the door."

ANGER 101

She glanced behind me and then her eyes met mine. As a consolation she offered, "Business class is not available, but I will check you in here." Then she asked me to put my first suitcase on the scale.

"Your luggage weighs two kilos more than is allowed," she said.

My worse fear was realized. I had to unpack right there. I don't want to. I make a plea with the truth; perhaps there are exceptions for charity so I asked,

"The suitcase is filled with donated books. I'm going to work at a school for orphans. May I take them, please? The school needs as many supplies as possible."

"If I had a penny for every time someone said they were bringing supplies for an African charity, I'd be rich."

Did she just say that? Oh my god. I could feel the pressure of anger building inside of me. Was she questioning my integrity?

"Imagine if when people told you that, they actually were telling you the truth. Wouldn't that be wonderful to know so many people are flying to Africa to help?"

The agent didn't acknowledge what I said. Instead, she stated, "The extra bag will be one-hundred fifty dollars. How would you like to pay for that?"

I told her I needed to unpack and figure out what books would stay behind. Inwardly, I was seething. I was disappointed I couldn't fly business class when I assumed I would. Being squashed between two strangers for almost twenty hours wasn't in my plan. Plus I was exhausted with all the preparation for this trip—arrange for my children, the pets, the garden, the house. I had collected all the donations and packed them. Then I had to stop along the freaking New Jersey Turnpike and fix the stupid bumper!

On top of it all, this flight was expensive with the coach airfare at $2000 paid for out of my own pocket. Taking what was happening personally, I wanted to scream. And cry. Those children at the school had nothing, and it broke my heart to think all of these supplies and books couldn't go to them.

My emotions must have been obvious because Martha said, "Lori, let's just move out of the way. Come over here." She pointed to the wall opposite the check-in counter. "Let's go through the luggage back there. I'll help. This happens all the time. We'll take out some weight, and you'll be fine."

We moved to the back wall where I stood, my body tight. I could feel the all of me rebelling. I looked around and saw the coach line people checking in and the lucky business class customers, too. Children were playing. Adults were talking. Everything was moving and changing in one way or another.

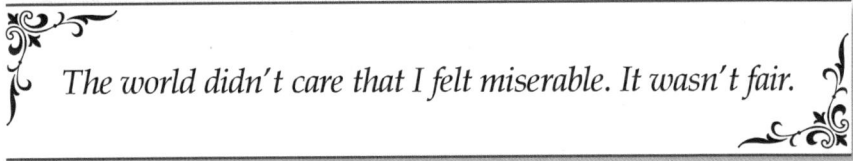

The world didn't care that I felt miserable. It wasn't fair.

Resistance—Then a Shift

I closed my eyes and instinctively went inside for a moment. I could feel my anger. My body was tight all over, with my chest and jaw holding the most tension. I wanted to fly business class. I wanted to be mad at the Ethiopian Airlines agent. I wanted to turn around and go home. I wanted to blame somebody. I didn't have an extra ounce of energy for anything else.

I closed my eyes and connected to my body and all that tension. I acknowledged my disappointment and anger. I heard an inner wisdom say, "Lori you are tired. You're exhausted. Just get the luggage right.

ANGER 101

Pay the extra fee. You can repay yourself with donations. When you get on the plane, you can relax, even in coach. It will be okay. What's important is to get to Uganda safely and have a successful visit. It's okay. It's all going to work out."

For a few seconds, I resisted. *I didn't want to feel okay.* I wanted to stay *mad*—but I couldn't. I knew what my inner truth told me was true, that everything was okay. Yes, I was disappointed and yes, I felt angry, but I surrendered to the fact that I would fly coach class, that I'd take fewer books with me, that I'd pay the extra baggage fee of $150 and somehow donations would reimburse me. I let go of both my expectations and the thought that the world was trying to stick it to me. I got it. It'd be okay and flying coach class would be fine, no big deal. The children in Uganda I was working for didn't even have food or a bed or medicine or even parents. So I actually felt grateful to being going back to Uganda. The words "a weight was lifted" were true for me.

I took a deep breath and opened my eyes, sensing the tightness in my body release. I felt a shift to openness. I felt relaxed. It *was* okay and so was I. Everything is and would be fine. In that moment, the energy in the airport seemed to shift, too, evidence of the emotional energy of anger transforming. I felt expansive and at peace, open for a new experience.

I bent over to join Martha as she unzipped the large, black REI duffel bag. We pulled out books one by one and shared sweet musings over the cute children books we found. We started a "this is going" pile and a "this is staying" pile. We chatted and joked, and within a few minutes, we unpacked what we thought was two kilos. We put the books on the "this is going" pile back into the duffel bag. Just as we were ready to zip it up, we heard, "Lori DiGuardi, please come to the check-in counter."

I looked up from my seat on the floor. It was the Ethiopian Airlines agent at the business class counter. I glanced at Martha. We both shrugged. Martha continued to close the bag as I stood up, brushed off the seat of my pants, and walked over.

"Ms. DiGuardi, I have a customer who flies business class regularly. He always has a seat reserved on this flight. I noticed he hasn't checked in and would have by now if he's flying with us today. Would you like me to call him to see if he's taking this flight? If he is not, I could upgrade you to his seat."

What a strange turn of events. I'm sure my face showed my shock. Was I supposed to tell her, "No, don't do that?" Of course not. I simply said, "If it's okay for you to call him, please do. I would greatly appreciate that."

She called him, speaking in what I assumed was Amharic so I didn't know what was being said. She hung up and then looked at me. "You're in luck. He isn't flying tonight. You can upgrade to business class and take his seat. Don't bother unpacking your luggage. I'll check it in with the extra weight. It's not a problem. How would you like to pay the four hundred dollar upgrade fee?"

The Beauty of Letting Go

The beauty of letting go to relax into the moment invites and reveals all the ingredients for miracles, perfection, and peace. It's like an immediate invitation for the best solution to manifest. Resisting the moment keeps the very thing you desire out of reach and gives power to what you're resisting.

Resistance is exhausting, nonproductive. When we let go of how we think things *should* be, our energy can freely flow into the next moment with grace and ease. Our prayers can be answered. Or something better than we imaged can be created.

ANGER 101

If we pray to divine beings to help while leaning against a closed door, their help can't get in. What we do to ourselves in fear and judgment is maddening—until we remember the secret. Let go and let god. Let go and go with the divine flow. Let go and know you will continue to breathe and your heart will continue to beat. Let go and allow grace and ease to be your rudder. Let go and trust. Let go and accept yourself in the moment.

> *Mostly, accept what your body is feeling and let it offer organic guidance. You can float without trying to float.*

Fear Wants Control

Fear tries to make every moment an opportunity to be in control again. Fear is diligent in telling us that things aren't okay now and they won't be okay later unless we control something, everything.

Without believing in fear, fear dies, so we can't blame fear for not wanting to lose its relevancy: it's fighting for its life in every moment. Fear wants to convince us that life is a struggle and dangerous. A struggle it will be until we are open to the truth of the moment, for resisting fear also gives it power.

Remember, what we resist grows stronger and takes control. It's as if fear is in the lighthouse looking out for us as we sail through the sea of life. It vigilantly perceives that everything looks like danger unless the wave is a safe wave, the boat is a safe boat, the breeze is a safe breeze, and the sun is in the same safe place in the sky. But if all things were the same as before, we'd go nowhere and never reach a new horizon. With even a hint of an impending cloud, rain drop, or wave, fear seizes the moment as if to say, "Alarm! Danger is imminent! You must do as I say or you'll die!"

Yet fear's unrelenting alarm decreases when letting go becomes a habit of surrendering, of acceptance, of presence. When we are aware and present, our perception shifts, and we see that the clouds can offer us much needed shade or beauty of the sky. The raindrop may be a refreshing cleanse or the answer to earth's thirst. Our heart's desire can ride in on a wave or the wave can create a resounding sound of peaceful aliveness. Or maybe sinking beneath the water will show us a whole other world of life's blessings.

When we surrender to the truth of what's happening within, our inner truth will always let us know what we need in the moment and open us up to something more. Even fear comes with body sensations and inner truth. When we drop into our bodies to listen and acknowledge what's happening inside, the stories that fear uses to frighten us give way. The energy transforms.

If you're struggling or resisting life, don't beat yourself up. If you feel emotional energy and override how you feel, don't beat yourself up. In part, how you respond to the moment and to yourself has to do with physiological shortcomings of the brain. That means beating yourself up is misdirected energy.

Our brains have grand canyons of neural pathways of conditioned behavior that tells us to resist, to judge, to ignore, to deny, to override. That's how our biology works. Blaming yourself for physiological shortcomings of your brain, whatever they may be, is misdirected energy better spent creating awareness and being patient and gentle with yourself while forming new habits and new neural pathways.

Most of all, be compassionate with yourself. If you find you're resisting the moment or how you feel, especially your anger, that's okay. Just accept that, too, and be open to the next moment.

ANGER 101

TIME FOR YOUR TRUTH

To start, practice at least one minute of grounding. (See Introduction for instructions.)

Then ask the following questions one at a time.

Be curious and be gentle. After asking each question, close your eyes and *feel* into each answer.

Write down your answers and insights, taking special note of those that yield the strongest sensations in your body. I recommend answering them by speaking into a voice recorder on your smartphone or other device. Then review them while practicing Embodied Awareness. (See Introduction for instructions.)

1) When do you allow yourself to do nothing, to just be?
2) When do you feel like you need to be in control? What's that about?
3) Where does struggle show up in your life? What do you not want to deal with? What do you resist?
4) Where or when in your life could you be extra gentle and compassionate with yourself?
5) Where in your life do you make great effort (that you aren't pleased with)? Is this effort familiar? How might "effort" be a habit? How would your life be different if you didn't have to exert so much effort? Who would you get to be?

SUGGESTED PRACTICES

Again, practice at least one minute of grounding and then take these actions:

- *** Take a minute to place your awareness in your body. Notice all the places you may be tense. Take a breath into those areas

and relax. Imagine creating space between every cell and molecule. Practice this through out your day.
- Think of something you're concerned about or have fear about, then check your body for tension. Become aware of any thoughts about what you "must" or "should" do in that situation. Repeat from *** in the list above. Hold the experience in your consciousness as you intentionally release any bodily tension. What is this experience like for you?
- Think of a task on your "to do" list that you don't want to do. Repeat from *** on the list and intentionally accept how you feel about this undesirable task. Breathe into acceptance. *Be totally okay with how you feel.* How might you allow your environment to support you?
- Acknowledge that you are worthy just because you are alive and needn't "do anything" to be worthy. How might you let go of trying to be worthy? What is possible if you let go of trying?
- Celebrate your willingness to surrender to truth.

An Enriched Life

Blessings from the Untruth

About six years ago, I joined an online dating site and used the headline "Alchemist Wanted."

To potential online suitors, this is the attention getter that, at first glance, shows what makes me stand out from the crowd. I had plenty of responses, just not the kind I'd hoped for. The most common one was "What's an alchemist?" I learned that if a man didn't know what an alchemist was, he wasn't one. Nor was he a guy willing to put a little effort into wooing me.

What was I expecting from that headline? To meet a man with optimism—a "glass half full" kind of guy who saw potential. And a man who knew what an alchemist was. At the very least, I hoped to connect with a man who would be fun to chat with on a first date. Ultimately, though, my best hope was to meet a man who led an alchemical life, like me.

Alas, I did not meet my alchemist on the dating site, but my brief membership experience was a positive one. I'm an eternal optimist. I am a lover of life, a visionary. And yes, I'm an alchemist, both by nature and by nurture. Give me crap and I will turn it into gold, almost without trying.

Not only was I born to be an alchemist, but my life experiences pushed me in that direction, too.

Making the Best of Circumstances

Here's the nurture part, though in this case, "nurture" is an ironic term to use. Growing up in a tumultuous and scary environment and into my early adulthood, I learned how to make the best of less-than-great circumstances. I got so good at turning every situation around that even the other people in my life probably thought their behavior wasn't so bad. "Lori seemed to be doing okay after all," they'd think. And I convinced myself that life wasn't so bad either. Anyway, it was all that I knew.

For each awful experience in my life, I could have given up and grown increasingly bitter. No matter how long it took me to recover from violence, heartbreak, or dysfunction, I always tried again. Eventually I was able to see the benefits of what seemed like repeated unlucky experiences. Finding the blessings that resulted from rotten life situations is a great way to let go of blame, regret, and resentment. And being a modern-day alchemist is highly transformative. Yet I know that while I was compelled to learn from each experience and transmute it quickly, I usually performed this alchemy *before* I dealt with the emotional aspects of the experience.

Here's what I learned: There are two alchemical processes required to move on from highly emotional experiences. One I was great at; the other not.

What challenged me was the process of transforming the emotional energy my body created. I didn't want to deal with all those messy emotions. I wasn't good at acknowledging and honoring how I felt, especially anger. Mostly, the emotions were immediately dismissed because of early childhood conditioning and, later, due to habit. Not wanting to deal with those messy emotions meant I was carrying around a big dark cloud into each experience and every relationship. Not wanting to deal with them also meant I was grappling with them *unconsciously* in every moment.

ANGER 101

Energy cannot be destroyed; it can only be transformed. So when we ignore our emotional energy, suppress it, or deny it, it stays right there—building, wreaking havoc, and seeking release. An accumulation of unresolved emotional energy turns into dense energy we call emotional baggage.

How do we transform emotional energy and baggage? By acknowledging and honoring it. We dive into its core and just "be" with it, before that energy can be released.

That's the process of transformation and how we connect with our inner truth. There's no expiration date on emotional baggage. It has an infinite shelf life. And it goes with us everywhere until it's transformed.

Nowadays, I consciously choose to hang out with my emotions before I transform my experience into the gold. I choose emotional and experiential alchemy—a process that totally transforms my experience.

> *Discovering the blessing of the experience and honoring all emotions is the ultimate alchemical jackpot.*

Vacation Utopia Until—

In July 2016, I went out of town for three nights with my friend Alana. She flew from the east coast into Tucson and we explored my new hometown for four days. We then flew together to California for a mini beach vacation in La Jolla, California.

On our third morning there, we decided to enjoy breakfast at the historic pink La Valencia Hotel. Our balcony table set with linens, fine china, and silver overlooked the garden and circular pool. We could see the Pacific Ocean just beyond the edge of the far-most balcony. I could hear the clinking of china, a murmuring hum of other patrons, and the sound of the waves and seagulls in the crisp seaside air. We sat back in luxury beaming at each other as we waited for our breakfast to arrive.

As I took my second sip of coffee, I noticed a call on my iPhone. Serena. She comes every Thursday morning to clean the house. Had she forgotten her key? Or perhaps she couldn't make it to the house this morning. I gently excused myself and walked into the privacy of the hotel lobby.

"Hola, Serena!"

"The TV is gone...your jewelry is missing...the back door was kicked in....what should I do?"

Burglary. Serena found a crime scene when she arrived at my house. My vacation utopia was immediately shoved aside by this shocking news.

I couldn't make sense of what I was hearing. My brain and body created a whirlwind of thoughts, emotions, and anxiety. In no time at all, I started to clear a pathway through the anxiety as I strained to see the upside of this burglary. Why was this happening?

My mind started to draw connections and possibilities that would result in positive consequences. Then I realized what I was doing and stopped. "Really? You're already trying to see the positive, and you don't even know what was stolen? You just went into shock yet you're trying to see the benefits?" In that moment, I realized what was happening reflected a lifetime habit.

There I was in a beautiful seaside open-air hotel lobby running through my life history in a nanosecond. In that moment, I realized that looking on the bright side of trauma my whole life had helped me survive and garner hope for another day. Most important, this habit of seeing the benefits of a traumatizing situation allowed me to circumvent the emotional energy and *not have to deal with my angry emotions.*

ANGER 101

As quickly as that insight popped into my awareness, I chose to shut down that habitual process. This time, I made a conscious choice to really experience the emotional energy I was feeling. Learning of the burglary overwhelmed me. I was creating a ton of emotional energy, which meant I was about to get a ton of practice.

I felt anger. I felt lost. I felt afraid. I wanted to hide. I experienced overwhelm—and disbelief. I took intentional breaths and practiced grounding myself so I wouldn't disassociate with the experience. I stayed in my body. Then after hanging up with Serena, I called a few people who could help me take steps to secure my house and my accounts as well as file a police report.

My safe haven and sacred sanctuary had been violated. With my computers stolen, all of my financial data had been compromised. So I spent the day closing my bank accounts and going online to change user IDs and passwords. My mind kept going to my jewelry—all of it, gone. I'd let go of most of my worldly possessions before I moved to Arizona and brought the few precious items remaining to Tucson. Now even more was gone—stolen.

Every time I habitually searched for a positive reason why the burglary happened, I dismissed it and put my attention into my body. As my ultimate safe haven and sanctuary, I wasn't about to violate myself by ignoring what was going on inside. Throughout my life, I felt much safer living in my intellect, but I knew the power of my life depended on being present with what I was *feeling*, not *thinking*. All day, I purposefully pulled my attention into my body so I could connect to all the emotional energy and sensations within me.

I knew that honoring me would be the ultimate silver lining in any life experience.

When I was finished on the telephone, I walked back to the balcony. Alana was eating her breakfast from a corner of the table while our waiter was bent over and mopping up the table and the floor. Before Alana could ask me who called, I exclaimed, "What happened?" As she was enjoying her breakfast, a seagull had swooped down and stole my omelet. In its get-away, the bird tipped over the juice glass and pushed the china onto the floor. Even my breakfast had been stolen!

Staying Grounded

While I spent time closing and changing accounts, Alana helped me stay grounded and focused in my overwhelm. And when I cried, she offered her warm embrace for comfort. Later in the afternoon, I asked Alana to find me chamomile essential oil, vanilla tea, Bach's Rescue Remedy, and something to eat—a request she honored. After she came back, she then made a request of me. Would I please stop with all the burglary remedial activities so we could go walk on the beach one last time before sunset? I agreed.

Right before I crawled into the sheets that night, I sat on the edge of my hotel bed with Alana next to me. She gave me a hug. I closed my eyes and checked in with myself, feeling the heavy energy of the day's events and emotions. I was physically and emotionally exhausted, yet I could feel I needed something. But what?

I closed my eyes and breathed into the areas of my body that held the emotional energy. My inner truth made it clear that I had to lighten up before bed. So Alana and I made silly videos using an app on my phone that placed masks and filters over our faces. We recorded our messages for three friends, laughing until we cried. Yes, I slept soundly that night.

Sense of Betrayal

The next day, as the plane approached the airport returning home, the burglary energy was strong, filling my mind with stories and thoughts.

ANGER 101

Not surprisingly, I was making the experience very personal. I felt betrayed. I had given up so much to move to Tucson. I wanted to hate the city. Besides, I was far from home and the people I loved.

My new home had betrayed me. Still, I knew I was supposed to be in Tucson. It wasn't logical. It didn't make sense. But I had heeded the call. And for what? To be violated again?

Then as the landing gear made contact with the earth, a great awareness came to me. Tucson hadn't betrayed me. Instead, strangers thought they needed what I had. They didn't know me. And if they didn't know me, they couldn't betray me. The betrayal I felt didn't come from the burglary. That old energy was seeking release from my body.

That simple acknowledgment shifted the energy for me a little. It allowed me to separate the *old* energy of betrayal from the *new* emotions of having my home violated. I still loved Tucson.

"Let's Do This"

The night before my flight home, I called a friend in Tucson because I didn't want to walk into my burglarized home alone. Michael said he would help. The end of his work day coincided with the arrival of my flight, so I met him in the Himmel Park parking lot a few blocks from my house. After a warm and solemn greeting, we drove to my place.

I took a deep breath as I put the key in the door lock. Though I was afraid to enter, I also felt eager to get it over with. Michael stood next to me as I opened the door. I could immediately see the TV was gone. Then we stepped inside together and made eye contact. I said, "Okay, let's do this."

As we walked through the rest of the house, I uttered in a monotone voice what I noticed. If I spoke calmly, somehow I'd feel better, right?

"My son's telescope is gone."

"My father's vintage lighter is gone. I loved that piece."

"They took my French cork screw. Oh my god, I can't believe it, but they took the bottle of tequila."

I hesitated to walk through the open bedroom door, but I did of course. Four empty jewelry boxes were scattered on my tainted bed. The bed pillows had been stripped of their cases and used for carrying the jewelry. My hand-carved cash box from the Congo sat in the middle of the floor with no sign of the international currency I'd kept in it. The doors and drawers of my dressers and armoire had been left open. This room, like the rest of the house, was in a state of chaos.

After a thorough walk through, Michael and I sat on the sofa and discussed what had happened. He invited me to stay at his place for the night and even the weekend if I wasn't okay to stay at my house. Yet, now that I was home, I didn't want to leave. So I thanked him and he left.

Each day over the next few weeks and at odd times throughout the day, I'd remember pieces of jewelry I no longer had; who had given it to me; from which country I had purchased them; which outfits I wore each piece with; which event I wore it to. With each recognition of loss—randomly at the grocery store, driving my car, lying down to sleep—I felt socked in the stomach again. A full week after the burglary, I realized that the burglars even took my U.S. Mail roll of postage stamps.

Each time I remembered something I no longer had, I'd make a note of it so I could add it to the renter's insurance claim. And each night before bed, I turned on every outside light and locked my bedroom doors. Whenever I left the house, I hid whatever had value to me. Plus I didn't sleep in my own bed for a week and before I did, I bought new pillows and cases.

Seeing the Bright Side—Not Yet

Over the next days and weeks, people tried to humor me, cheer me, and get me to see the bright side. I felt both appreciative of their consideration and also angry. The anger made sure I honored my choice of being with the emotions of the burglary. This time, I didn't want to shortchange myself and go right for the light at the end of the tunnel. I knew the tunnel was a heavy path, but it was the path I was called to take.

The anger reminded me to stay the course. When a friend said, "You don't have to hide your wallet just to walk up the block," I responded, "That may be true, but I'm not ready to go there yet. I'm allowing myself to be with whatever arises within me. And right now I want to hide my wallet."

Shock and fear were having their way with me, *and I accepted that.* At the same time, I had awareness that material stuff is temporary and I didn't have to hide anything. But my conscious choice was to allow myself to be in the trenches with these human emotions and honor them with love and compassion. I'd move through the loss and violation of the burglary organically. I knew blessings were waiting for me, and I was in no hurry to reach them.

> *This time around, I would experience life more consciously than ever. I chose total transformation.*

Black, White, and Gray

Learning to turn every trauma into a blessing is a great quality to have. Life gave me ample opportunity to practice seeing the upside to every downside. It's as if I'm adept at the Hermetic Principle Law of Polarity that says (in part) if you travel north long enough, you'll find yourself moving in the direction of south. Thus, nothing is black or white; everything is black, white, and gray.

Growing up in a volatile environment taught me to be extra sensitive to the energy dynamics of the circumstance and the moods of others. When I sensed my father in a rough mood, I'd stay out of his way and escape getting hit. When my mother was emotionally overwhelmed, I learned to stuff my own emotional needs so they didn't push her over the edge. I stayed away from my step-father when he was drinking, and I left the house when only the two of us were home. When my first long-term boyfriend felt particularly vulnerable and insecure, I could change my plans and give him my full attention so he wouldn't abuse me out of jealousy.

As a child and young person, being sensitive to the needs of others helped me remain safe.

An Effective Leader

Acknowledging the needs of others has also made me an effective leader. People know I genuinely care how they feel, what they think, what's going on in their world. I'm present and engage with others. People feel seen by me because I do see them deeply. They feel good around me because they do matter to me. As others sense my vulnerability, it's easy for me to establish a sense of trust. These strengths are powerful in my personal relationships and in my professional work. When people open their hearts and minds to me, they know they are safe in doing so.

In those early years, rather than come out fighting (gaining the wrath of those who seemingly had power over me), I kept a low profile and tried to bring energy into balance. I worked hard at calming people down—for my own safety and the peace within my childhood home. I applied logic in conversations to convince people there was another, more peaceful way to address the situation at hand.

To protect myself, I also worked hard at defending myself in a way that didn't seem defensive and didn't come with an ounce of being offensive. I learned excellent communication skills so I could dialogue productively with even the most unaware and narcissistic people. As a diplomat and a peacemaker, I learned to confidently create a peaceful atmosphere and diffuse a situation.

In Service to Others

Being in service to others is beautiful. After all, we're all in this world together. In the early years, most of my service work was fueled by an unconscious yet compelling need to save the world. My devotion to humanitarian, environmental, and animal rights organizations was propelled by more than "it's the right thing to do." Underlying that was a lifetime of unresolved emotions seeking acknowledgment and release.

When emotions, judgments, and beliefs hide in the shadows of consciousness, they drive us to project them on to external targets. That's why we often go about trying to fix, heal, and save the world at large. Similarly, emotional insecurity has driven many leaders to rise from the masses as CEOs, dictators, and politicians.

What we don't own in ourselves will own us.

"You Need *You*, Lori"

I got my first real clue in this regard when I coached with Chris Liaguno and he said, "When you start giving yourself what *you* need, you will feel less compelled to fix others."

At the time, I didn't buy in to that completely, though a quiet whisper inside me said, "You need *you*, Lori." Almost every one of my family members depended on me to be the "man" of the family. I couldn't see how *they* would change if *I* changed. I admit; I was a bit defensive in my role as the family fixer upper, but when I hear the truth, I hear it. What Chris said resonated deeply.

When it comes to humanitarian, environmental, and animal organizations, well, many a people's shadow selves have created success in the world. There's nothing wrong with that. My shadow self created powerful change for the world at large through these types of organizations. If I were still projecting my needs onto the world, I'd still be working around the clock, literally, by donating my money and time to saving whales, local dogs and cats, orphans in Africa, children in poor villages, political campaigns, police and military organizations, nonprofits for breast cancer, heart disease, lung cancer, and various environmental organizations. How exhausting just to think about all of them!

I don't know *how* I contributed so much, but I do know *why* I did it. Though I needed *me*, I projected my need onto everything else. Here's why. When we ignore our own needs, our subconscious and unresolved issues get us to do super-human feats until we break open. That's when we see ourselves as the needy inner children who are screaming for attention and love.

Went into High Alarm

Back in 1999 when I learned about the school in Uganda, I was just starting my divorce process and feeling emotionally raw and needy. Leading the charge were the repressed emotions from my childhood—neglect, rejection, abandonment. When I heard the Ugandan school created for orphans and underprivileged children was about to close, my whole being went into high alarm.

I decided to help the school's children because being a child needing support, a voice, and a safe environment yet not having any of that

ANGER 101

resonated with me. I took on the challenge of keeping the school open for the children. For three years, I financially supported the school by myself. The needs continued to grow, but my income did not. Still, I sent money to this Uganda school because the people there had come to depend on me. I felt responsible not only for the underprivileged children there but the entire school community. What a familiar condition—putting others' welfare above my own.

When I saw I couldn't help them as they needed, I felt awful and even selfish. At that time, I was still making myself wrong, ignoring my inner truth, and not setting boundaries as the energy of anger would have me do.

I felt great dissonance with what was happening. There I was supporting an African community while I was going through divorce with two young children. I was alone, but I needed support, too. Something was *trying* to happen, and it did.

With plenty of prayer, meditation, and contemplation, my awareness shifted from "I can't support the school" to "I don't have to support the school on my own." What a step. Obviously I needed to take care of my children and myself, and somehow the school in Uganda would be okay. I'd help if and when I could. Once I felt solid in that understanding, my energy shifted. Then it happened.

I started getting calls and emails from other people who wanted to know more about the school. Soon, they were donating money, and my support changed into a leadership role. By listening to my truth, accepting it, and doing what I needed, the world came to my side. As long as I ignored my feelings and my needs, the world would, too.

> *The world starts within us. It's our mirror. So when we honor ourselves, the world honors us, too.*

TIME FOR YOUR TRUTH

To start, practice at least one minute of grounding. (See Introduction for Grounding Exercise instructions.) Then ask the following questions one at a time. Be curious and be gentle. After asking each question, close your eyes and *feel* into each answer.

Write down your answers and insights, taking special note of those that yield the strongest sensations in your body. I recommend answering them by speaking into a voice recorder on your smartphone or other device. You would review them while practicing Embodied Awareness. (See Introduction for instructions on Embodied Awareness.)

1) Do you notice that you circumvent "negative" feelings by jumping right into "positive" feelings or not feeling anything at all? Or perhaps you create more negativity? Describe your process.
2) Bring to mind a challenging life experience, trauma, or other "negative" experience. List and describe some of the personal qualities that came from that experience.
3) What positive qualities do you have that you were born with?
4) What positive qualities do you have that are both nature and nurture (both questions 2 and 3)?
5) Are you consciously aware of any emotional baggage that you have? If yes, describe what you know about it.

SUGGESTED PRACTICES

Again, practice at least one minute of grounding and then take these actions:

- Commit to stop habitually defending your truth or how you feel, including saying "I'm sorry."
- Commit to do something fun this week. Notice how the experience influences your regular weekly experiences.
- Allow yourself to be supported. Choose a situation in your life and ask someone to help you with it.
- Celebrate you, because you deserve it without having to earn it.

Starting Over

The Power of You

September 2014 marked the beginning of a new major cycle in my life—I was starting over.

As always, the old has to die to make way for the new. Therefore, that September started with feelings of loss. A few months earlier in June, the younger of my two children had graduated from high school, which meant both of my children were adults and living away from home. At the time, my daughter lived in upstate New York and my son in Scotland. Their public school was replaced with college and university.

As quickly as their lives changed, mine did too, and especially my role as their mother. No longer would September come with an incredible busyness that included back-to-school and sports events. No more getting up at six in the morning to wake up the kids and prepare a hearty breakfast, something I loved doing. Most important, for the first time in twenty years, I would not celebrate my September birthday with my children.

That September required redefining my life, my roles, and my desires. My biggest change was moving *me* to the top of my list. *I* was my list. After twenty years of being an afterthought to myself, I became the main character. Yet being number one seemed strange and unfamiliar. Grocery shopping was only for me; laundry was only mine; programs on the barely watched TV were only for me. Breakfast, lunch, and dinner—a meal for one.

And with the absence of my children, the silence in my house was profoundly deafening.

A September Birthday

Along with loss, I also felt excitement to create new dreams. When waking up, I'd lie in bed wondering, "What do I want to eat? How do I want to spend my time?" Because I was planning to sell the house, move, and build my career, that required a lot of me. But beyond that was a big unknown. And first, I had a September birthday to attend to.

For that reason, I traveled to Sedona, Arizona—a location chosen deliberately with a little help. A few months earlier, I had an astrology session for a birthday solar return with Susan Baroni. She said, "The solar return birthday trip is the most powerful catalyst in astrology." The sun and planets at the time and location of our birth define our natal chart, which remains the same during our lifetime. What changes is *where we are* on our birthdays. So choosing where to spend a birthday "does not change the aspects the planets are in, but it will change which [astrological] houses [the planets] land in," she said. In effect, that creates the potential for cosmic support (or lack thereof) for our upcoming goals.

Susan requested my top three goals and then went to work. She contacted me a few weeks later for our session, saying I was really lucky. "Most of my clients want to spend their birthdays in Sedona but rarely does that location support their goals. For you, it's the best location in all of North America and Europe. How does spending your birthday in Sedona sound to you?"

I had visited Sedona a few years earlier at Christmas and loved it. Since the time my children were four and two, they spent every other

Christmas with their dad so I traveled during the holidays to escape the loneliness. Since then, I've learned to travel not because of a custody schedule but because of natural evolution of life—a first. So naturally, going back to Sedona for my birthday sounded great, especially knowing this beautiful place would support my goals.

Life Priorities Supported

My life's priorities at that time were all about me, of course. I wanted support as I showed up more heroically, honorably, and powerfully than ever before. My upcoming year's goals were 1) selling the house and moving, 2) expanding my coaching, speaking, and writing career, and 3) affording my lifestyle through all of that change. In our session, Susan told me that not only would my birthday solar return in Sedona support those areas but that location would bring good energies to all my other astrological houses as well.

When she got to the relationship house, she mentioned something about Saturn being in the eighth house. As she reported, "It looks like you'll be given an opportunity to get into your power with your lover. He might have some unusual sexual requests. Remember, it's your choice to say, 'Okay, I'll try that. Handcuffs?' Or if you might say, 'No, I don't feel comfortable doing that.' If he does something that's a power play—if he handcuffs you and you feel disempowered, for example—take notice. If you feel you're one-hundred percent in your power and it's fun, then that's different.

"But again this is not to punish you; it's to help get you to be comfortable in your power. When you leave here [through death], you're leaving here alone. It's not going to be about him. It's going to be about what you learned here."

Of course, I was particularly curious about that "handcuff" part of the astrology session. After all, I was single and hadn't dated for a few years.

Also, I wondered what made her use handcuffs in her explanation. Was she using it as metaphor or did she have psychic abilities?

Well, I soon found out. Around the time of my session with Susan, I met David. He was a wonderful person and very direct. In bed, he went for what he wanted and took charge if I didn't say otherwise. Our magnetic physical chemistry fueled his assertiveness in intimacy. Because he was a safe and honorable man, I could tell him what worked for me, what did not, and what I preferred. If I spoke up, he listened. If I didn't, he took charge. With him, I had plenty of opportunities to set boundaries and learn what being powerful meant to me in a healthy relationship.

This time around while in relationship, I connected with the healthy emotional energy of anger within me in its infancy. "Oh, no Lori, you don't like that. You'd better tell him." When he made requests, I checked in with myself before I answered. "No, I'd prefer not to do that. Let's try this instead." Or I'd say, "Okay, yes." While with David, I connected more deeply with my inner truth. He made it easy for me, but since relationship with a man was my kryptonite, I still practiced diligence, courage, and intention. I didn't want to fall back into old habits—that is, allowing the man's desires and needs to be more important than mine.

> *For the first time in a romantic relationship, I was heroic, honorable, and powerful for myself. I could expand into my greater truth and authentic power.*

Every Moment a Learning

The following year, September 2015, I scheduled another birthday solar return reading with Susan. This one took me to Glastonbury, England, where I had a magical week in the land of Arthurian legend.

No handcuffs were part of the astrology reading this time. And for my birthday in 2016, I reached out to Susan again. After a few weeks had passed and I hadn't heard from her, I called.

A man answered. "Hello, this is Dennis."

"I'm calling for Susan about a birthday solar return I purchased from her."

"Oh, yes, she's good at astrology. I am her trustee."

"Trustee?"

"Yes," he said. "And I'm her executor, too."

Susan had transitioned. I felt surprised, saddened. From Dennis, I got the impression she had not been well for a while. In her transition, was she able to look back at her history and be pleased at how authentically powerful she was? I wondered. I hope she passed knowing that what she'd come to learn she had learned well.

What I have repeatedly learned in every moment from gentle to traumatic is this: Until our time on earth is over, every moment gives us an opportunity to start over.

We needn't wait till our kids leave the house. We needn't wait to use our power wisely. We are not bystanders. Rather, we are the creators and visionaries in our lives. Every moment is the perfect time to connect with our inner truth. Every choice is a chance to use our authentic power.

Never Too Late

Even if you ignored inner truth most of your life (as I did), you can start living a more powerful life of emotional integrity *right now*. It's never too late to connect with the power within and let your inner truth lead

ANGER 101

you to your promised land. Allow your inner truth of anger to show you that the *inside of you* is asking for acknowledgment and change. Allow the wisdom that's always within you to show you how to be honorable, heroic, and powerful.

> *Commit to yourself and to your healthy emotional energy of anger so it may guide you along the journey of being a sacred, self-loving bitch.*

TIME FOR YOUR TRUTH

To start, practice at least one minute of grounding. (See Introduction for instructions.) Then ask the following questions one at a time.

Be curious and be gentle. After asking each question, close your eyes and *feel* into each answer.

Write down your answers and insights, taking special note of those that yield the strongest sensations in your body. I recommend answering them by speaking into a voice recorder on your smartphone or other device. Then review them while practicing Embodied Awareness. (See Introduction for instructions.)

1) What cycle of life is alive for you now? Where in your life are you starting over? What is new and what is dying?
2) What are three top priorities in your life right now? How are you honoring them? What support do you have/need for them?
3) What recent experience brought forth more empowerment for you? What made the experience empowering? What inner truth did you honor?

4) On a scale of 1 to 10, with 1 being "not so good" and 10 being "great," where are you at honoring your inner truth of anger these days?
5) On a scale of 1 to 10, with 1 being "not so good" and 10 being "great," where are you with being authentically powerful? What connection exists between your answer for number 4 and 5?

SUGGESTED PRACTICES

Again, practice at least one minute of grounding and then take these actions:

- Practice Embodied Awareness. When you are solidly planted in your body ask, "What do I need right now?" Is there anything you need to give yourself right now? Is there anything your body or your heart wants for you right now? If so, put down this book and honor yourself. Start the next moment engaged with your truth.
- Affirm the knowing that you are beautiful, worthy, and perfect just as you are. Feel that truth within your body.
- Commit to your top three priorities from Time For Your Truth number 2. Keep reminders about your commitment to these priorities in auspicious places. Check in with yourself in the morning and before bed to see how you honored these priorities.
- Celebrate the power of you.

Conclusion

The Truth of Your Existence

Unless you are a 10 on the 1-to-10 scale of self-realization or unless you can claim Buddhahood, you can more deeply embrace the truth of your existence.

The potential to expand into greater authenticity is your best friend. And that potential exists with each breath.

As you read these words, STOP. Now close your eyes and take a breath. Connect with yourself and your inner truth in this moment. Feel your body sitting or standing, and connect with the floor, with the earth. Feel the majesty of your body and beingness. Feel the hum of aliveness in the core of your being.

Breathe in, knowing you are a blessing and an exquisite being of the universe.

Breathe in, knowing that you have a right to how you feel.

Breathe in, knowing how you feel is the truth of your existence right now.

Embrace These Truths

Say "yes" to the miracle of you. Smile. Explore what's happening inside. Feel the sensations of your body. Let the energy of you be in intimate communion with the world in every moment. *You are that powerful.*

How do you feel right now? What sensations are alive within you? Perhaps your tummy is rumbling, your lower back is sore, or your chest feels tight or wide open. Maybe you have goose bumps, or you feel light and expansive after reading the paragraph before this one. Possibly your mind is taking the lead, and your thoughts are bouncing around.

Whatever thoughts or images are filling your head, notice them. Then take a breath and refocus your awareness into your body. What are you experiencing inside? What is happening for you? What do you feel?

Say hello to your gut. Thank your heart for beating. Know that your liver is doing liver things well. Allow your lungs to connect the outside world with your inside world and vice versa. Imagine your blood flowing through all of you, carrying nutrients, oxygen, and love to every part of your body. Layers of sound surround you. Your eyes are interpreting black marks on a light background, and your brain gives this experience meaning.

In this very moment, the power of *you* is sustaining and enriching your one precious life. All of that has an energetic experience. *That is your truth.* It goes beyond words, stories, thoughts, habits—just pure sensation. It's that simple. Notice without words.

Practicing Embodied Awareness

I suggest my clients practice this—Embodied Awareness—when they are cooking, lying in bed, chatting, doing anything anytime they want. Practicing it can be effective even when watching a movie. A typical movie creates feelings of joy, anger, fear, curiosity, anticipation, and more. So watching it gives plenty of opportunity to explore how energetic sensations feel and move in our bodies as we experience emotional energy.

The more you deliberately practice *acknowledging* how you feel when you are moving through the day, the more apt you will be to *connect* to your inner truth at those times you need to most. That's why Embodied Awareness is powerful. Taking the process one step further is acknowledging what's happening in the body and honoring the inner truth. I call that the Acknowledgment Cycle.

Acknowledgment Cycle

This cycle is the process of connecting with the sensation of emotional energy, acknowledging its presence, and letting that energy tell you what you need, then honoring that wisdom. Sometimes the healthy emotional energy of anger simply wants you to rest. Other times it may tell you to say, "No, thank you."

Your inner truth of anger may want you to leave a situation or a relationship, to speak up and take action. When you acknowledge your inner truth of anger through Embodied Awareness, that cycle always leads you to a self-loving, soulful, fulfilling potential.

So use the Acknowledgment Cycle to honor yourself, for it's not about blame, judgment, or violence. Simply ask, "How do I feel? What do I need? How do I give it to myself?" It's a simple and powerful process.

True Power—An Inside Job

Each time we intentionally bring awareness to what's going on inside, we breathe into our authentic power. With practice, we start making choices that better honor what we value. Our truth is priority. And with practice, being in touch with our truth and especially our anger begins to be as natural as breathing. Saying "yes" to ourselves no longer takes effort or courage.

> *When we stand in our authentic power and embody the truth, there is no need to defend ourselves.*

Defending Yourself

When you find you are defending yourself to yourself or anyone else, take this as a cue to practice Embodied Awareness and the Acknowledgment Cycle.

We don't need to defend how we feel; we need only to honor how we feel. Defending our choices provides a good indication to slow down and take a break, go inside, and see what's happening within. When we defend ourselves to others, we are subconsciously resisting our inner truth.

Yet our inner truth doesn't need us to defend it. If we're willing to live in integrity, our inner truth is there to be acknowledged and honored. It will always be patiently waiting for us to love ourselves.

The moment we stop being compelled to defend ourselves is when we experience true freedom. Life flows with grace and ease when we honor ourselves and live with emotional integrity. We're living the life of a healthy bitch.

Embodying my awareness and practicing acknowledging my inner truth has become a religious practice for me. It's the only way I could connect to my healthy emotional energy of anger and not ignore it after so many years of struggle. Acknowledging our healthy emotional energy of anger is the miraculous way our bodies' wisdom keeps us on track with what's important to us. It helps us thrive. After all, we are on earth to live our precious lives with integrity and fulfillment. By so doing, we enter the land of freedom and joy.

Honoring ourselves is the only way to wholly experience heaven on earth.

Sometimes we break *down* before we have a break *through*. Each time I get closer to a deeper truth, something happens to strip me of false beliefs even more. When I find myself struggling, I know that there is potential for my authentic power to expand.

For those of us who learned so many untruths about ourselves, growing into emotional integrity is *not* easy. We live with conflict, unhappiness, and struggle till one day we break open and bits of the truth are revealed. Then we have to let go of what *isn't* true so we can start over.

As the relationship with ourselves changes, so it changes with everyone and everything else. Susan Baroni, bless her soul, was right when she said that in our relationship with self and the world, each decision reflects how we choose to use our power.

Your Heart as a Guidepost

A true guidepost along the journey of using our power wisely is our heart—the interpreter of soul language. I have heard many people say, "I followed my heart, and it was a mistake." "I should have known better than to have followed my heart." "Whenever I follow my heart, I always get hurt." Or, "I had a change of heart."

Yet if you follow your heart, you follow inner truth, which is never wrong.

Why do so many people fear following their heart? It has to do with the imposter of truth: fear. You can be fooled into believing the voice of fear is really the voice of the heart. *Fear learns the language of your heart and uses it well.*

Be not fooled, for your heart will never ask you to worry, doubt, or be insecure. It will never question your intentions with "But what if…?" You may have a change of mind but not a change of heart, for your heart will never lead you to dishonor. Never.

Your infinite soul is the keeper of wisdom. To hear your heart and heed its wisdom, you must be in your body, feel your truth, and listen fully. People with a strong intellect who see life as a logical scientific process have minds that can be called "masterful." In fact, that was my story.

But when the mind rules, it squeezes out the soul's truth that the heart tries to radiate. Within that strong intellect is fear persuading you that it's the voice of truth and heart. Don't buy into that. Your head can help carry out the soul's wisdom, but on its own doesn't have a chance.

If you find you're not thriving as you'd like, that you are struggling more than you'd like, that you aren't as fulfilled as you'd like to be, you *can* start over immediately. That is the power of you.

Fulfillment is the Goal

When our thoughts, words, and deeds honor our inner truth, we are in integrity; we are our most powerful selves. When we are in integrity, we experience fulfillment. If our soul and Embodied Awareness tell us one thing yet our heads and subconscious tell us another, we have inner conflict. Inner conflict equals a lack of emotional integrity. When emotional integrity is missing, life fulfillment is a goal that remains elusive from our lives.

As much as we want to be in service to others, unless we are first in service to *ourselves*, we cannot do our best or most powerful work. If we give our lives over to others, their needs, their demands, their requests, and ignore our own truth, we do so at our own peril.

Living this way is not sustainable. A healthy wholesome life requires healthy wholesome boundaries. The healthy emotional energy of anger will always guide us in setting healthy boundaries. Without boundaries, without prioritizing our own needs, and without *self-love*, the world will never be satisfied from what we give it—nor will what the world gives to us be satisfying either. Effortful demands won't stop.

Both men and women have much to gain by committing to self-honor. Yet without practice, the concept could never become a reality; it could never become a personal truth. In fact, when anger is inappropriately expressed or repressed, it becomes a detriment to the individual and community.

However, when the inner truth of anger is honored, the person living in emotional integrity and authenticity contributes to a healthier society. That's why I believe that honoring our anger would do a world of good. The world would know more peace if we as individuals had more inner peace. But what actually happens? When we don't listen to our inner truth, we are at odds with ourselves.

As my coach Chris Liaguno said, "May we see the conflict inside of ourselves before we project it as a war on others."

An Enriching Journey

I started my story with sharing how I was taught at the age of three that being me is wrong. I followed that for many years. Fortunately, the untruth I'd adopted didn't stand a chance to continue indefinitely. My subconscious mind was relentless in its control, and the struggle of my life became a habit. But my heart and soul whispered through every moment, "Lori, there is more."

> *I've spent my life hungering for that "more," and the journey to find it has enriched my ability to live a powerful life of service.*

Playing doctor was a toddler's effort of being in service to another and acknowledging my true wisdom within. I wasn't able to listen to my cousin Steven's heart that day, but I have spent over thirty years learning how to listen to *mine*.

Today, my life's work involves leading people to the wisdom of their bodies, their hearts, and their souls, because I am listening to mine. I am a superhero of the soul, and yes, one heroic, honorable, and powerful bitch.

TIME FOR YOUR TRUTH – is now.

A Prayer for the Remembrance of Truth

Oh Dear Omnipotent God,
The Beingness of All,
The Love, Lover, and Beloved of All Creation,
The Truth Beyond Comprehension,
The Deepest Inspiration and Beat of Our Hearts,
Dear Precious God,
Please bless us, each of us, through which your essence flows,
Bless us with the realization of our highest divine potential,
Bless each of us so that we know the miracle that we are,
Bless us with the courage to embody unconditional love for ourselves,
Bless us with the knowing that for fear, there are no guarantees strong enough and for love, none are needed,
Bless us with the fortitude to love fear into oblivion,
Bless us so that each breath we breathe is an expression of Love,
Dear Blessed All That Is,
Please bless us with the absolute knowing that each of us is perfection and worthiness,
Bless us so that we know we are worthy of Love simply because we exist,
Bless us into knowing that who we are just as we are, is enough,
Bless us with freedom from inner-conflict so that self-violation in thought, word, or deed, is extinct, obsolete, unheard of,
Bless us so that as we become a blessing to ourselves, we are also a blessing to All others,
Oh Dear Sweetest Love,
Bless us with Divine vision, so that we see our sacredness in each other,

Bless us with Awakened Holiness so that we can love ourselves by loving the other,
Bless us so that our experience of each and every person, place, and thing, is a call to Love,
Bless us with inner peace so that we create a world of outer peace,
Please Dear Brightest Star of our Infinite Universe,
Please bless us with the Knowing that We Are You, You are Us, and We are One.
Bless us by reminding us of the Truth of Our Existence,
Bless us.
Thank you.
Amen.

Acknowledgments

I'm grateful that I made the commitment to write this book and had the courage, strength, and support to see it through to completion.

I feel indebted to TEDx Tucson for giving me the opportunity to speak on its magnificent stage. The commitment to write this book was birthed as a result of the audition. For the audience members who spoke to me, your feedback reiterated the importance of sharing our truths. We all need to know that we matter and that we are not alone in our pain.

And that leads me to Holocaust survivor and human rights activist Gerta Weismann Klein. Nine years ago, I heard Mrs. Klein speak in Philadelphia. Her story and message—that our pain is to be a source of strength to help others—inspire my life's work and the writing of this book.

My coach Chris Laiguno provided unwavering support and belief in me. He helped me honor my truth and stay grounded in Embodied Awareness when I was most uncomfortable with writing.

My editor Barbara McNichol not only welcomed me to Tucson, she helped me feel safe and confident as a new author of delicate emotional material. She helped lighten my chapters so they were easier to read, and she did it so gently.

Lulu.com and its self-publishing packages came with clear instructions and the people there held my hand through a process that can be nerve shattering for a new author.

Alana Coppola, my soul sister, is a one-woman cheerleading team. She kept me going with her fire and love through out the writing of this book. A few years ago after attending one of my workshops, Alana said in her south Philadelphia accent, "Lor, you need to do a TED talk!" Look what's happened since!

Dearest Thane Kraut listened to my struggles all along the timeline of this book. His vision of me helped me expand into who I am.

My sisters Sharon and Michelle have been with me through most of the stories in this book. Their unconditional love and belief in me kept me company during a lonely writing process.

To my children Carolynne and Patrick, you are the reasons I consciously chose to stop the ancestral prophesy of victimhood and abuse once and for all. Your lives made me birth this new approach to living—one in which I was called to be heroic, honorable, and powerful for you and for myself, no matter what.

I'm grateful to everyone who was part of the traumas and joys in my life. There's not a single experience I regret. We all agreed to come to earth to learn from and teach each other in the ways our souls agreed upon. Thanks to all for keeping your soul agreements with me.

And for everyone dear to me I haven't mentioned, I'll give you a hug next time I see you. Thank you for loving me.

About the Author

This all-around Superhero of the Soul helps people live their greatest potential—"the key to living my own life soulfully."

Lori DiGuardi is a transformational personal development coach, award-winning speaker, and author of *Anger 101: The Healthy Approach to Being a Bitch*, also the title of her TEDx talk. The title represents Lori's struggle with anger, how it formed due to abuse, and how she became liberated from its grasp.

She grew up in single-parent household on welfare and food stamps, which inspired her to reach beyond her limits from an early age. Her 25 years as a leader in United States, Europe, and Africa repeatedly revealed an essential life truth—that fulfillment and harmony increase when individuals connect with their own inner truth. Sharing this has become the cornerstone of Lori's passion and mission as a coach, speaker, and author.

In 2010, Lori had the distinct honor of earning Rotary International's Service Above Self Award for her volunteer work in Africa. She proudly adds this credit to her bachelor's and master's degrees and her International Coach Federation certification. She also holds a black belt in Tang Soo Do karate.

You can learn more about Lori's soulful work at www.loridiguardi.com.